playing with
PATCHWORK & SEWING

Nicole Calver

- **6 Blocks in 3 Sizes**
- **18 Exciting Projects**
- **Skill-Building Techniques**

stashBOOKS®

an imprint of C&T Publishing

CW00656276

Text and photography copyright © 2020 by Nicole Calver

Photography and artwork copyright © 2020 by C&T Publishing, Inc.

PUBLISHER | Amy Barrett-Daffin

CREATIVE DIRECTOR | Gailen Runge

ACQUISITIONS EDITOR | Roxane Cerda

MANAGING EDITOR | Liz Aneloski

EDITOR | Karla Menaugh

TECHNICAL EDITOR | Linda Johnson

COVER/BOOK DESIGNER | April Mostek

PRODUCTION COORDINATOR | Tim Manibusan

PRODUCTION EDITOR | Alice Mace Nakanishi

ILLUSTRATOR | Aliza Shalit

PHOTO ASSISTANTS | Rachel Holmes and Gregory Ligman

INSTRUCTIONAL PHOTOGRAPHY by Nicole Calver, unless otherwise noted; lifestyle photography by Estefany Gonzalez and Kelly Burgoyne and subjects photography by Diane Pedersen of C&T Publishing, Inc., unless otherwise noted

Published by Stash Books, an imprint of C&T Publishing, Inc., P.O. Box 1456, Lafayette, CA 94549

All rights reserved. No part of this work covered by the copyright hereon may be used in any form or reproduced by any means—graphic, electronic, or mechanical, including photocopying, recording, taping, or information storage and retrieval systems—without written permission from the publisher. The copyrights on individual artworks are retained by the artists as noted in *Playing with Patchwork & Sewing*. These designs may be used to make items for personal use only and may not be used for the purpose of personal profit. Items created to benefit nonprofit groups, or that will be publicly displayed, must be conspicuously labeled with the following credit: "Designs copyright © 2020 by Nicole Calver from the book *Playing with Patchwork & Sewing* from C&T Publishing, Inc." Permission for all other purposes must be requested in writing from C&T Publishing, Inc.

Attention Copy Shops: Please note the following exception—publisher and author give permission to photocopy pattern pullout pages P1 and P2 for personal use only.

Attention Teachers: C&T Publishing, Inc., encourages the use of our books as texts for teaching. You can find lesson plans for many of our titles at ctpub.com or contact us at ctinfo@ctpub.com or 800-284-1114.

We take great care to ensure that the information included in our products is accurate and presented in good faith, but no warranty is provided, nor are results guaranteed. Having no control over the choices of materials or procedures used, neither the author nor C&T Publishing, Inc., shall have any liability to any person or entity with respect to any loss or damage caused directly or indirectly by the information contained in this book. For your convenience, we post an up-to-date listing of corrections on our website (ctpub.com). If a correction is not already noted, please contact our customer service department at ctinfo@ctpub.com or P.O. Box 1456, Lafayette, CA 94549.

Trademark (™) and registered trademark (®) names are used throughout this book. Rather than use the symbols with every occurrence of a trademark or registered trademark name, we are using the names only in the editorial fashion and to the benefit of the owner, with no intention of infringement.

Library of Congress Control Number:2019949572

Printed in China

10 9 8 7 6 5 4 3 2 1

Acknowledgments

Mom. My best friend and #1 fan since day one. The women who watched my kids, a lot, hand stitched my bindings, came over to help press things. And baste quilts. And hold things while I took pictures. I honestly, truly, could not have done this without you. Thank you. #MyMomIsBetterThanYours

Tan and Al, I couldn't ask for better best friends than you girls, and better sisters, well that's not even possible. Thank you for supporting me on this adventure and all the ones before. You get a quilt, and you get a quilt and quilts forever!! But not right away; I need to send them to mom for binding!

Dad, thanks for always keeping a smile on my face, for all the times you picked the boys up from school so I could work, and for helping me the first time I tried spray basting a quilt, I haven't gone back to pins since!

G, you've always been there with your encouraging words and sweet heart. I can't thank you enough for it all. I'm 100 percent positive I wouldn't be here right now if not for you.

Alice, thank you for believing in me and my ideas so much. For picking me up when I fell and assuring me that I really could do this. You were right. I totally did this! But not without help, and yours was invaluable.

Becky, thank you so much for being my real-life, in-person sounding board! Your advice and offers of help truly meant the world to me. I'm lucky to call you friend.

To my awesome team at C&T who made this possible, especially my amazing editor Karla, thank you so much!!

And Shawn, for every time I called you from your studio to mine to see if this looks right. And does this make sense. And should I move this here. And I need this, can you take me to get it. A thousand times thank you. I love you. Forever.

DEDICATION

For my boys.

To Sam, who was the most extraordinary reason behind making my first quilt and who continues to inspire my creativity with his every day.

And to my sweet Max, whose favorite book is his favorite because a quilt is given as a gift. And Max says there is no better gift than that!

Contents

Using This Book | *You will know to look for more information in the Glossapendium! whenever you see a word or concept highlighted, like this:* **Nine-Patch Units** *(page 112). The concept will be highlighted only once within a pattern at the point where it would be useful.*

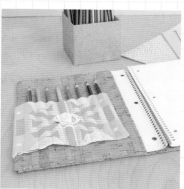

Pfft, that's totally a word. It's obviously a Glossary and a Compendium smooshed together. This is the place to come and learn the terminology and techniques used in the book. I'll also share some of my favorite tools!

INTRODUCTION

There are no limits to what you can sew when you are supposed to be doing something else!

My house is living proof of that. Every time my little sister comes over, I tell her not to worry about taking off her shoes. Because I've said it so often, she automatically replies with, "The floors need to be washed anyway!" Yes, I live in a constant state of floors that need to be washed, never-ending mountains of laundry, and the general chaos and mess that comes with two little boys under nine and their two-year-old dog. But there's sewing! There's always time for sewing!

I try my best to sew at least once a day, even if only for a few minutes. Quilts are my favorite to sew, and I sew a lot of them. We are nothing if not an epic home for a quilt fort! That being said, my husband is showing concerns about how many more quilts we can fit into our house. I'm pretty sure the answer is always "at least one more"!

So I do understand the need for a small or fast sewing project to whip up when something surprises you, like the last day of school or Christmas. Such sneaky days that advance far more quickly than regular days. I hope you'll find something here that helps when a holiday sneaks up on you. I've included a wide variety of projects so I'm sure there's something to be made for everyone, or all for yourself.

No judgment here, friends. Just have fun!

I've divided the chapters into four parts, the first being how to make the featured block. Easy start. Following are three projects that use the same block, but in different sizes—some easy, others maybe a little more difficult.

But don't limit yourself to using the blocks with the projects listed. Mix it up!

That New York Beauty pincushion in Chapter 6 would make a perfect coaster! The coasters in Chapter 3 could easily be sewn together to make a pot holder or mug rug. Or maybe you think that awesome cutlery wrap from Chapter 1 would make a great pencil roll but with hexies instead of simple patchwork! That's what I want to see—how you make the projects all your own. That's where the fun is!

Now go! The floors can always be washed tomorrow!

—Nicole

1

Simple Patchwork

It's a patchwork picnic party!

I love a good picnic! Whether it's at a park, on the beach, or even in our living room, there's something about spreading out a quilt and snacking on a smorgasbord of goodies that makes life so much more fun! The world needs to picnic more and work less in my opinion, so why not the perfect picnic package to help? Yep, that's right. I'm saving the world here, friends, one picnic at a time! So, this picnic perfect package has the must-have patchwork picnic quilt and a super-handy market sack that will hold both the food and the quilt! And why not throw in a little cutlery wrap as well, which of course has its own special pocket in the market sack!

SIMPLE PATCHWORK BLOCK   8

Mega Project
Picnic Party Quilt   9

Medium Project
Double-Strap Market Sack   12

Micro Project
Tuck-and-Roll Cutlery Wrap   22

SIMPLE PATCHWORK BLOCK

Simple Patchwork block

Photo by Nicole Calver

Simple Patchwork blocks will always have my heart—they're the perfect, easy-to-use block for most people starting their quilty journey. And despite the simplicity in design, the results you can get with color and layout placement is staggering!

Block Essentials

This is what is needed to make the sample block. All individual sizes are included with the actual projects.

An assortment of squares: All the same size

Simple Patchwork Block Construction

Seam allowances are ¼˝ unless otherwise noted.

Block Assembly

1. Arrange the squares. For the sample, I've used 4 rows, each with 6 squares, to make a rectangular block. But your patchwork could have any number of squares in a row, and could be rectangular or square.

Play around with the fabric until you're satisfied with the layout. I like to cut out more squares than I need. That way I can find that just-perfect combination, and the leftovers can be used in a different project! FIG. A

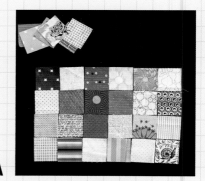

A

2. Sew the squares together, ***chain piecing in rows*** (page 115). Press the seams in each row in opposite directions so the ***seams nest*** (page 116) later on. Follow the arrows for pressing direction. FIG. B

3. Sew the rows together and press the seams open.

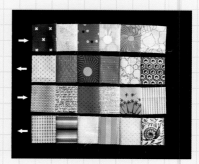

B

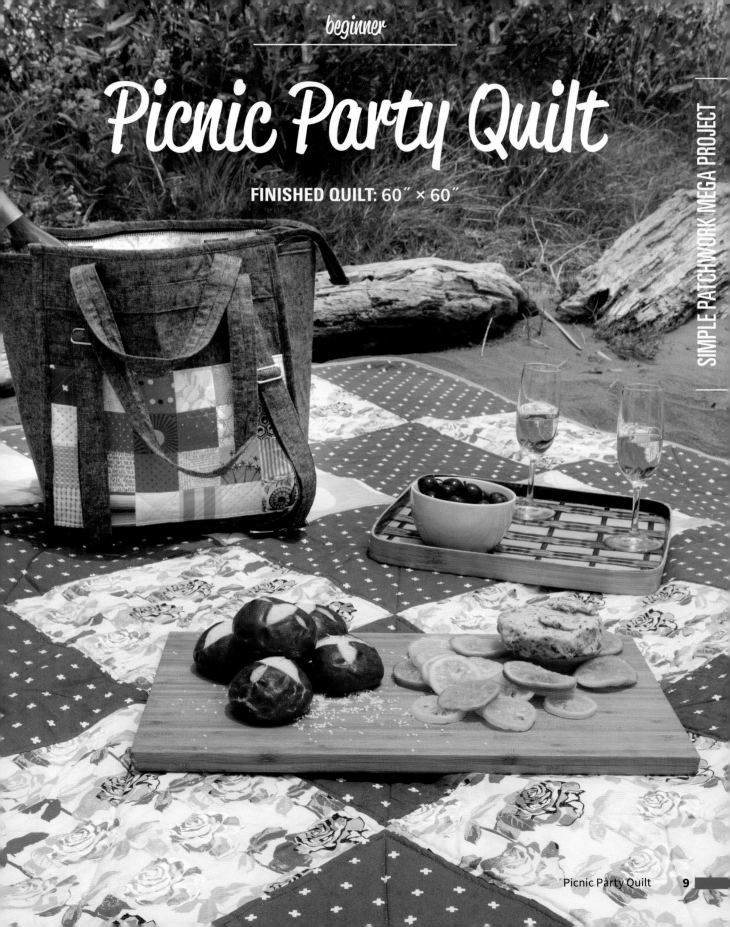

Picnic Party Quilt

FINISHED QUILT: 60″ × 60″

Skill Builders

Matching corners

Curved quilt corners

Quilt finishing

Bias binding

Sometimes simple is best. This is definitely the case with picnic quilts. There's something about a simple patchwork quilt that begs to be pulled out at the beach or along the river and just enjoyed for its simplicity. And let's be honest, it also can be really great to finish up a project quite easily in a day! Pair simple patchwork and large-scale blocks, and you have a quilt top that can be made in under an hour!

Materials

Fabric requirements are based on 40˝ width of fabric unless otherwise noted. Please note that these fabric requirements leave no room for error; adjust accordingly.

Dark gray: 2 yards

Light gray birds: ¾ yard
(I fussy cut the bird fabric to feature a bird in each square. If you plan on fussy cutting, you may need extra fabric depending on the size of the fabric repeat.)

Floral: 1¼ yards

Binding: ⅞ yard

Backing: 3¾ yards

Batting: 68˝ × 68˝

Cutting

Dark gray: Cut 5 strips 12½˝ × width of fabric; subcut 13 squares 12½˝ × 12½˝.

Light gray birds: Cut 2 strips 12½˝ × width of fabric; subcut 4 squares 12½˝ × 12½˝.

Floral: Cut 3 strips 12½˝ × width of fabric; subcut 8 squares 12½˝ × 12½˝.

Backing: Fold the length of yardage in half; cut across the width at the fold.

Construction

Seam allowances are ¼˝ unless otherwise noted.

Assembly

Assembly is easy for this one! This quilt is just one big block. See Simple Patchwork Block Construction (page 8).

1. Arrange the squares in 5 rows, 5 blocks per row. Alternate the placement of the dark gray squares as shown in the quilt assembly diagram (next page).

2. Sew the squares into rows. Stitch the rows together to complete the quilt top.

Finishing

1. Sew the backing rectangles together lengthwise using a ½″ seam allowance. Layer with the batting and quilt top, and quilt. See *Quilt Finishing* (page 117).

2. Before binding curve the corners. To do this, I used a dinner plate as a template and just cut off all four corners. At any given moment, there is enough dishware in my sewing room to serve a six-course meal, just so I can find that perfect curve!

3. Because of the curves in the corners, prepare *double-fold bias binding* (page 113). Use a 29″ square to make 260″ of 2½″ double-fold bias binding.

Now bind as desired and go have a picnic! Or wait!! You should definitely stick around for the rest of the picnic party projects!

Quilt assembly

Double-Strap Market Sack

FINISHED BAG: 13½″ tall × 12″ wide × 9″ deep

FINISHED BLOCK: 12″ × 8″

Skill Builders

Matching corners

Bag construction

Installing a zipper

Installing strap sliders

The idea for the Double-Strap Market Sack came about while walking home with a bag full of groceries and kicking myself for not thinking to bring a backpack instead of my usual market bag. While standard market bags are handy, traveling long distance on foot with 30 pounds of groceries on your shoulder is not a happy way to start the day. So why not have convertible straps that can go from over-the-shoulder to backpack straps in the blink of an eye! Throw in an insulated lining and not only does it keep the groceries cold on the way home, it can double as a picnic bag!

Materials

Fabric requirements are based on 40˝ width of fabric unless otherwise noted. Fat eighths are 9˝ × 21˝.

Assorted scraps: 24, minimum 2½˝ squares for patchwork pocket (This is a great chance to highlight some fun fussy cuts!)

Pocket lining: 1 fat eighth, print or solid

Black linen: 1¾ yards for bag exterior, straps, and seam binding (This could be a quilting cotton or similar.)

Other supplies

Fusible fleece: 1 fat eighth

Insulated lining: 45˝ wide, ¾ yard, for bag lining (Try Insul-Shine by The Warm Company or other similar product.) Note that if you use a product that is different in width, see the cutting instructions for the exact size cuts and calculate accordingly.

Fusible woven interfacing: 20˝ wide, 1½ yards (such as Pellon SF101 from the bolt)

Double-stick fusible web (optional): 24˝ wide, 1¼ yards (I used Lite Steam-A-Seam 2 by The Warm Company.)

Zipper: 18˝ length

Metal slide adjusters: 4 adjusters, 1¼˝

Rectangle rings: 4 rings, 1¼˝

Zipper foot

Denim 90/14 sewing machine needles: 2 needles recommended (I found sewing through the insulated lining dulled my needle quite quickly.)

Water-soluble pen: Or other nonpermanent marking tool

Fabric glue: For basting

Seam roller (optional)

Note | The way this bag is constructed makes it super-simple to switch out one type of lining for another. Maybe you don't need the bag to be insulated, or maybe you prefer a more rigid bag. Whatever you choose, the construction and piece sizes remain the same. I've kept mine simple, choosing to use only the exterior fabric and the insulated lining. The insulated lining was actually from an old insulated bag that had ripped, so I took it apart and repurposed it! You may choose to skip the insulation and use a stiff interfacing in between the exterior and lining. Or how about canvas for the exterior and quilting cotton inside? Quilting cotton outside and in, with foam in between? The possibilities are endless!

Cutting

Assorted scraps: Trim 24 scraps to 2½″ × 2½″ squares.

Pocket lining: Cut 1 rectangle 8½″ × 12½″.

Black linen

- Cut 1 strip 12½″ × width of fabric; subcut 1 rectangle 12½″ × 37½″ for main exterior.

- Cut 1 strip 9¾″ × width of fabric; subcut 2 rectangles 9¾″ × 14¼″ for sides.

- Cut 8 strips 3″ × width of fabric for straps.

- Cut 4 strips 1½″ × width of fabric for seam binding.

Fusible fleece: Cut 1 rectangle 8½″ × 12½″.

Insulated lining

- Cut 1 rectangle 12½″ × 37½″ for main exterior.

- Cut 2 rectangles 9¾″ × 14¼″ for sides.

Fusible woven interfacing: Cut 6 strips 3″ × length of interfacing.

Double-stick fusible web (optional)

- Cut 1 rectangle 12½″ × 37½″ for main exterior.

- Cut 2 rectangles 9¾″ × 14¼″ for sides.

Construction

Seam allowances are ¼″ unless otherwise noted. Topstitch ⅛″ from the edge.

Making the Pocket

Refer to Simple Patchwork Block Construction (page 8) for this section.

1. Using the 2½″ squares, make a Simple Patchwork block of 4 rows, 6 squares per row.

2. Following the manufacturer's instructions, fuse the wrong side of the patchwork block to the fusible fleece. Quilt if desired.

3. Right sides together, join only the long edges of the patchwork block and the pocket lining, leaving the sides open. Turn right side out and press. Topstitch along the top edge. Set aside. FIG. A

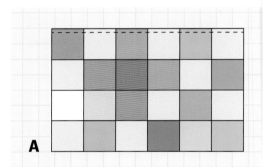

Preparing the Straps

1. Sew the 3″ strap strips together with *diagonal seams* (page 113).

2. Following the manufacturer's instructions, fuse interfacing to the entire length of the pieced strap. To start a new piece of interfacing, overlap the previous piece by about ¼″.

3. Cut the strap fabric into the following lengths:

2 strips 12½″ for the strap holders

1 strip 35″ for a short handle

1 strip 66″ for a short handle

2 strips 76″ for the backpack straps

4. Fold each strap in half lengthwise, right sides together, and stitch the long edge.

> ### TIP
> I like to press the seam open now with a seam roller. I find that when it's turned right side out it's easier to press flat if this is done first.

5. Turn the strap tube right side out. To do this, pin a safety pin to one opening of the tube. Carefully feed the pin inside the tube and push it through to the opposite opening. As it pushes through, it's turning itself right side out. FIG.B

6. Press all the straps with the seam running down the center. *Topstitch* (page 116) along both long sides.

Preparing the Seam Binding

1. Sew all 1½˝ *seam binding* (page 114) strips together with *diagonal seams* (page 113).

2. Cut the binding into the following lengths:

2 strips 10˝

2 strips 38½˝

2 strips 20½˝

1 strip 3˝

3. Press into the seam binding.

Preparing the Main Panel and Side Panels

1. If you use …

… *fusible web to attach the insulated lining,* fuse the pieces wrong sides together following the manufacturer's instructions. For all other

interior/exterior combinations, you will need to *baste* (page 112) around all 4 sides with an ⅛˝ seam allowance.

… *the exterior fabric and lining only,* baste the wrong sides together.

… *an exterior fabric, lining, and stiff interfacing (optional version),* sandwich the interfacing between the exterior and interior rectangles, right sides out, and baste as above.

2. Follow the same process for the main panel and both side panels.

3. Mark the center point of both long edges of the main panel.

4. Sandwich the top edge of a side panel in a 10˝ strip of seam binding and topstitch in place along the bottom of the seam binding. Repeat with the second side panel. FIG.C

5. Mark the center point of the bottom edge of the side panels. Mark ¼˝ from each bottom corner.

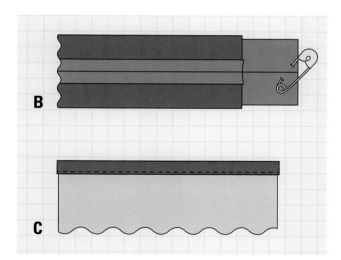

B

C

Attaching the Holding Straps

1. Pin a 12½″ strap 1½″ from the top edge on the front of the main panel.

> **TIP**
>
> If you are using insulated batting, use clips instead of pins to hold the pieces together. Pins will leave permanent holes in certain types of insulated batting.

2. Topstitch a 1″ square box on the top strap, starting ½″ from the left side. Stitch an X to reinforce the box.

3. Topstitch another 1″ box 3¼″ from the left side, and reinforce with an X. There should be a 1¾″ gap between the boxes.

4. Repeat Steps 2 and 3 on the right end of the strap.

5. Repeat Steps 1–4 on the bottom edge of the main panel. FIG. D

Attaching the Short Handles

1. Decide which end of the main panel will be the bag front. Place a mark 11½″ down from the top and 1¾″ in on both sides.

2. Feed both ends of the 35″ strap through the 1¾″ gaps in the strap holder, making sure the seam is facing the bag and the straps are not twisted. Pull both ends down so the outer edge of the strap and the bottom is aligned with the 11½″ mark. There should be a 16″ length of strap above the top edge of the holding strap.

3. Sew a 1″ X-reinforced box on each strap, right below the holding strap.

4. *Bar tack* (page 116) across the width of the strap ½″ above the holding strap.

5. Starting at the bottom of the 1″ boxes, top-stitch the strap edges down that are below the holding strap. FIG. E

6. On the opposite side of the main panel, feed the ends of the 66″ length of strap through the 1¾″ gaps in the holding strap, making sure the seam is facing the bag and the straps are not twisted. Pull both ends until they meet the ends of the other strap. There should be 16″ length of strap above the top edge of the holding strap.

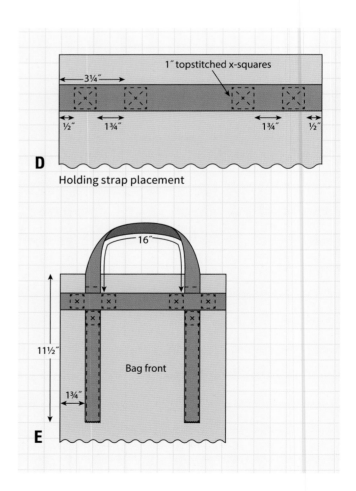

D Holding strap placement

E

7. Slide 2 rectangle rings onto each end of the 66″ strap. With the rectangle rings out of the way, zigzag across the bottoms of the straps where they meet. This junction will be hidden by the front pocket.

8. On both straps, sew a 1″ X-reinforced box 12½″ down from the top edge of the main panel. Mark 1″ from the bottom of both boxes. Slide 1 rectangle ring on both sides so it sits in between the box and the mark. Sew another 1″ X-reinforced box starting at the mark.

> ### TIP
> When sewing near hardware like rectangle rings, I like to use my zipper foot. It's made to get up close and personal with zippers, so why not with hardware!

9. Measuring from the other end of the bag, repeat Step 8 with the other 2 rectangle rings.

10. Repeat Step 3 on the 66″ length of strap, making sure to topstitch the straps down in between the 4 rectangle rings on what will be the bottom of the bag. **FIG. F**

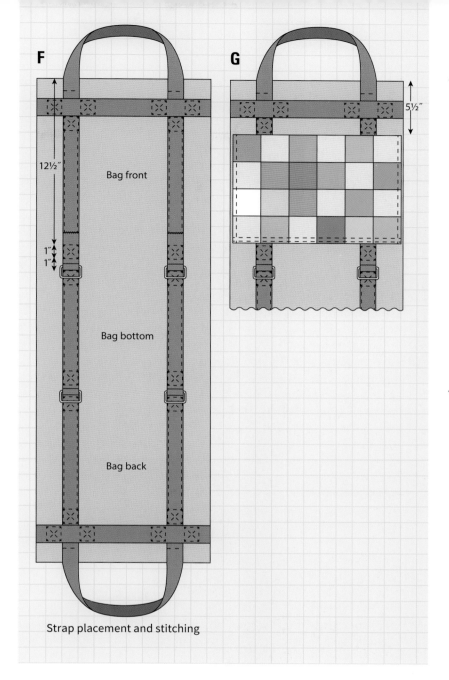

Strap placement and stitching

Attaching the Pocket

1. Right side up, position the pocket on the bag front (the side where the straps meet) 5½″ from the top edge.

2. Topstitch along the bottom edge of the pocket with a ¼″ seam allowance and then again with a ⅛″ seam allowance. Baste the sides in place. **FIG. G**

Bag Assembly

1. Wrong sides together, match the center mark of the main panel with the center mark of a side panel and clip in place.

2. Starting at the center mark, lockstitch and sew until the corner mark, then lockstitch again. **FIG.H**

3. Remove the bag from the sewing machine and adjust the main panel so it lines up with the long side of the side panel. Sew from the corner mark up to the top, lockstitching at the start and end. The side panel should end ½˝ from the top edge of the main panel. **FIG.I**

4. Go back to the center mark and repeat Steps 2 and 3.

5. Repeat Steps 1–4 on the opposite side of the bag with the second side panel.

6. Sandwich both edges of the bag with the 38½˝ lengths of seam binding and clip in place. **FIG.J**

7. Starting on the bottom edge of the bag, glue baste both sides of the binding in place. Maneuver the corners so they miter nicely and glue. Remove all the clips and topstitch the binding in place, making sure to catch the binding on both sides. Trim off any excess at the top. Gluing all the seam binding in place may seem like a hassle, but it makes it infinitely easier to sew, especially around the corners. Stitch slowly!

Side panel Right side

Body Wrong side

Center

H

½˝

Corner mark

I

TIP

If the corners are being troublesome, give them a tiny snip to ease. Just make sure you don't snip too far!

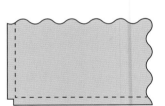

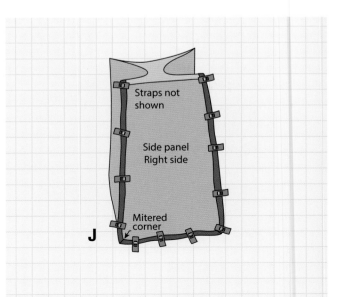

Straps not shown

Side panel Right side

Mitered corner

J

Attaching the Zipper

1. With the zipper face up, line up the start of the zipper with the edge of the bag. Wrong sides together, sew the zipper in place with a scant ¼″ seam allowance. Unzip the zipper and align the other side of the zipper on the other side of the bag and sew. FIG.K

2. Fold one short end of both pieces of 20½″ seam binding under ½″ and press. Starting with the folded edge of the binding, line it up with the start of the zipper and sandwich the binding around the raw edge of the zipper and bag. Sew in place, continuing down to the end of the zipper. Repeat on the other side. FIG.L

3. Measure how much seam binding is needed to cover the zipper end, add 1″, and cut from the 3″ piece of binding. Fold ends under ½″, and sandwich the zipper end inside the seam binding. Sew in place. FIG.M

4. Hand stitch any open ends of the seam binding closed with a simple whip stitch or ladder stitch.

Attaching the Backpack Straps

1. Feed the ends of the 76″ strap through the 1¾″ gaps in the holding strap, making sure the seam is facing the bag and the straps are not twisted. They will sit in front of the short handles. FIG.N

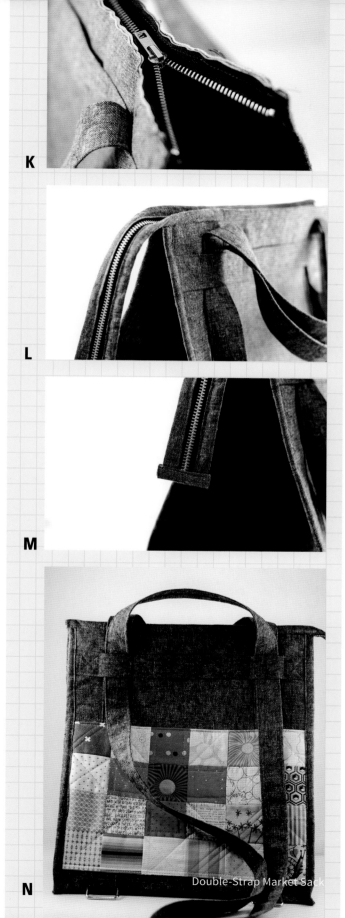

K

L

M

N

Double-Strap Market Sack

2. Feed 1 strap end at the left through the top slot in a metal slide adjuster, over the middle bar and out the bottom slot. This will now be referred to as the front strap. Now feed the end under the rectangle ring at the bottom of the bag front, and up toward the slider again. FIG. O

3. Loosen the part of the front strap that sits over the middle bar of the slide adjuster and feed the end of the strap over the middle bar again. Pull 1¾˝ of the strap through the slide adjuster and fold it back on itself. Fold the end under ¼˝. FIG. P

4. Sew along the bottom edge of the strap, making sure not to catch the front strap. Sew an X-reinforced rectangular box along the bottom edge for strength. FIG. Q

5. Repeat to add a slide adjuster to the strap on the right side of the bag front.

6. Repeat Steps 1–5 to add the second strap to the back of the bag.

Note | These straps are identical on the front and back of the bag. The ones on the back are for use as a backpack, and the ones on the front are there to hold the quilt. Both front and back are used when lengthened as over-the-shoulder style handles for a traditional market/grocery bag.

O — Slide adjuster / Rectangle ring

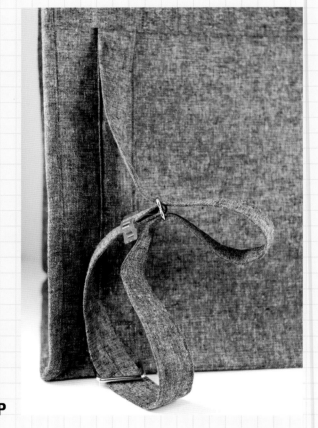

P

Q

Now throw some potato salad and sandwiches in there and a bottle of lemonade, slide your picnic quilt in the front strap, and you're ready for a picnic party! Oh wait!! Not yet, you should definitely make the next project in this chapter first!

Tuck-and-Roll Cutlery Wrap

FINISHED BLOCK: 6″ × 18″
FINISHED WRAP: 10″ × 18″ open

Skill Builders

Matching corners	Using bias binding
Using mesh fabric	Making strip sets
Using seam binding	Quilting

While eating finger foods on a picnic is swell, eating potato salad with your fingers is not. Yikes! How about we whip up a fast cutlery roll so no one dips their fingers in the salads, okay?

Materials

Fabric requirements are based on 40˝ width of fabric unless otherwise noted. Fat quarters are 18˝ × 21˝; fat eighths are 9˝ × 21˝.

Assorted quilting cottons: 12 squares 10˝ × 10˝ for variety for patchwork

Gray linen: 1 fat quarter for exterior and lining (This could be a quilting cotton or similar.)

Fusible fleece: 45˝ wide, ⅜ yard

Mesh: 44˝ wide, ¼ yard (If you can't find mesh at your local fabric shop, just do what I did and cut up a mesh laundry bag! You can find mesh laundry bags in dollar stores or from Ikea for next to nothing!)

Floral: 1 fat eighth for front flap

Pink solid: 1 fat eighth for flap lining

Black: 1 fat quarter for bias binding and seam binding

Cording: 50˝ (I used ⅛˝ parachute cord, but any pretty kind will work!)

Water-soluble pen: Or similar nonpermanent marking tool

Cutting

Assorted quilting cottons: From *each* of the 12 squares, cut 2 rectangles 1½˝ × 9˝ (24 total) for patchwork.

Gray linen

• Cut 1 rectangle 10˝ × 18½˝ for interior.

• Cut 2 rectangles 2½˝ × 18½˝ for exterior.

Fusible fleece: Cut 2 rectangles 10˝ × 18½˝.

Mesh: Cut 1 rectangle 7˝ × 19½˝.

Floral and pink solid: From *each*, cut 1 rectangle 5½˝ × 17½˝ (2 total) for flap.

Black

Cut in the order given:

• Cut 1 strip 1½˝ × 21˝; trim to 1½˝ × 19½˝ for seam binding.

• Cut 3 or 4 diagonal strips 2˝ wide.

Construction

Seam allowances are ¼″ unless otherwise noted.

Patchwork Panel

Normally when making **four-patch units** (page 112) I would press the seams to one side or the other to nest them. However, when pieces are this small, I press the seams open. In this case, use whatever method you are comfortable with.

> ### TIP
> When making a project with a lot of small pieces, it's sometimes easier to make strip sets. Strip sets are perfect when all the fabrics stay in the same order, but they can also work in random placement if there are enough of them. Which makes it perfect for this project! Not all of the pieces need to be strip set. For this project I fussy cut the black-and-white striped squares and set them into four-patch units individually so I could better manipulate their placement.

1. Randomly join 1½″ × 9″ patchwork rectangles lengthwise together in pairs for **strip sets** (page 112).

2. Cut each strip set into 6 segments 1½″ wide. There will be more than you need, but this allows for more options.

3. Sew strip-set segments into four-patch units. Make 27.

4. Arrange the four-patch units into 3 rows, 9 units per row. Sew four-patch units together into rows and press the seams open. Sew the rows together and press the seams open. **FIG. A**

Exterior Panel

1. Sew an exterior strip 2½″ × 18½″ to the top and bottom of the patchwork panel. Press away from the patchwork. **FIG. B**

2. Wrong sides together, follow the manufacturer's instructions to fuse the exterior patchwork panel to a fusible fleece rectangle.

3. Quilt if desired and round the corners. I used a small glass as my template and cut all 4 corners around it.

Interior Panel

1. Fuse the lining to the second fusible fleece rectangle wrong sides together. Quilt if desired. Don't round the corners yet.

2. Prepare ½″ **single-fold seam binding** (page 114) with the 1½″ × 19½″ strip.

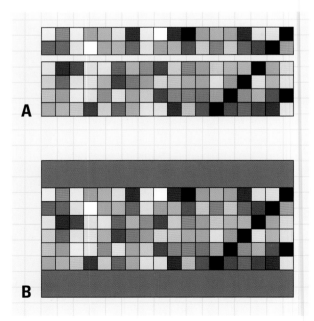

A

B

3. Sandwich one long edge of the mesh in the seam binding. *Topstitch* (page 116) along the top and bottom edge of the seam binding. FIG. C

4. With the interior panel right side up, place a mark 6″ up from the bottom corners on both sides in the seam allowance. Round the bottom corners.

5. Place the mesh right side up on the interior panel with the top edge of the seam binding at the marks. Stitch the sides of the seam binding in place, just in the seam allowance.

6. Mark the center point of the bound mesh edge. Sew a vertical line from the top center mark to the bottom of the mesh, lockstitching at the top.

TIP

Sewing the mesh can be tricky if you're not careful. It's not easy to mark a straight line to sew on, either! I solved this problem by running a perpendicular strip of masking tape from the center mark. I placed a couple of horizontal pins down the line and stitched just to the side of the tape.

---

7. Continue sewing vertical lines on the mesh 1½″ apart, working from the centerline out. Baste the edges of the mesh with an ⅛″ seam allowance, following the corner curves. Trim the excess mesh. FIG. D

TIP

Don't need a cutlery wrap? Sew some extra vertical lines in the mesh and use it as a pencil or marker roll! Or fill it with makeup brushes for the perfect gift!

---

8. Right sides together, layer and press the 2 cover flap rectangles together. Round the bottom corners. Stitch around both sides and the bottom edge, leaving the top edge open. Turn right side out and press.

9. Topstitch ⅛″ and again ¼″ from the edge around the 3 sewn sides. Mark the center of the flap's top edge in the seam allowance.

10. Mark the interior panel's center top point in the seam allowance. Round the top corners.

11. Right sides up, lay the cover flap on top of the interior panel, aligning their center points. Baste the cover flap in place with an ⅛″ seam allowance. FIG. E

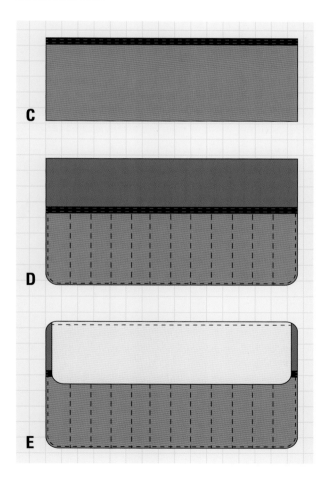

C

D

E

Wrap Assembly and Finishing

1. Before proceeding, prepare at least 66″ of **double-fold bias binding** (page 113) using the 3 or 4 bias strips cut from the black fat quarter.

2. To assemble the wrap, layer the interior and exterior panels *wrong sides together*, and baste around the perimeter with a ⅛″ seam allowance.

3. With the interior facing up, machine stitch the bias binding in place. Take care not to catch the sides of the cover flap in the binding. **FIG.F**

4. With the exterior facing up, mark the center of the right side. Fold the cord in half and place the fold on this mark; the loose ends will face towards the inside. Stitch the cord in place on the binding seam allowance. Shortening your stitch length will make it easier to catch more of the cord. **FIG.G**

5. Fold the binding over to the exterior side and hand stitch down. Add some fun beads to the ends of the cord, or even just tie a couple of knots to finish.

Now fill it up with some picnic cutlery, and wrap, tuck, and roll! Or if you fold it in thirds so it lies flat, it's the perfect size to slide into the front pocket of the Double-Strap Market Sack (page 12)!

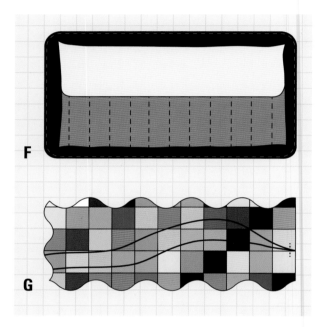

F

G

2

Grandmother's Puzzle

Not your grandma's bed-in-a-bag!

Okay, let's get real here for a minute. You remember back when you were little and you had the whole bed-in-a-bag deal and thought it was just totally rad?! Your My Little Pony bedspread matched the My Little Pony pillowcase, which also matched the My Little Pony decorative pillow! You know what I'm talking about. It was so cool! And then you grew up. And now, while it would still be cool to have that same My Little Pony bed-in-a-bag set for my queen-size bed (my husband begs to differ), wouldn't you rather have a perfectly bespoke bed-in-a-bag set? One that you've made with cotton fabrics to match your style, and your taste? Yes, please!

GRANDMOTHER'S PUZZLE BLOCK 28

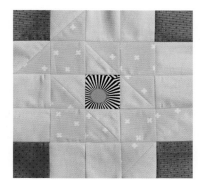

Mega Project
Grandiose Grandma Quilt   29

Medium Project
Granny Shams   32

Micro Project
Puzzling Patriarch Pillow   36

GRANDMOTHER'S PUZZLE BLOCK

From afar, the Grandmother's Puzzle block looks like a tricky one to put together. But I've made some minor adjustments to the way the block is constructed that make it super-simple to make at any size.

Block Essentials

This is what is needed to make the sample block. All individual sizes are included with the actual projects.

Aqua:
- 8 squares for background
- 4 squares for half-square triangles

Yellow:
- 4 squares for block
- 4 squares for half-square triangles

Pink: 4 squares for corners

Focus fabric: 1 square for fussy cut center

Grandmother´s Puzzle Block Construction

Seam allowances are ¼″ unless otherwise noted.

Block Assembly

1. Using 4 aqua and 4 yellow squares, make 8 *half-square triangles with the 2-in-1 method* (page 111). Square up the half-square triangles to the same size of the other squares in the block.

2. Arrange the squares and half-square triangles in 5 rows of 5 as shown.

3. Sew the squares and half-square triangles together, *chain piecing in rows* (page 115). Follow the arrows for pressing.

4. Sew the rows together to complete the block. Press the seam allowances open.

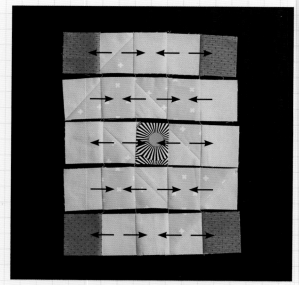

Repeat pressing direction for all rows.

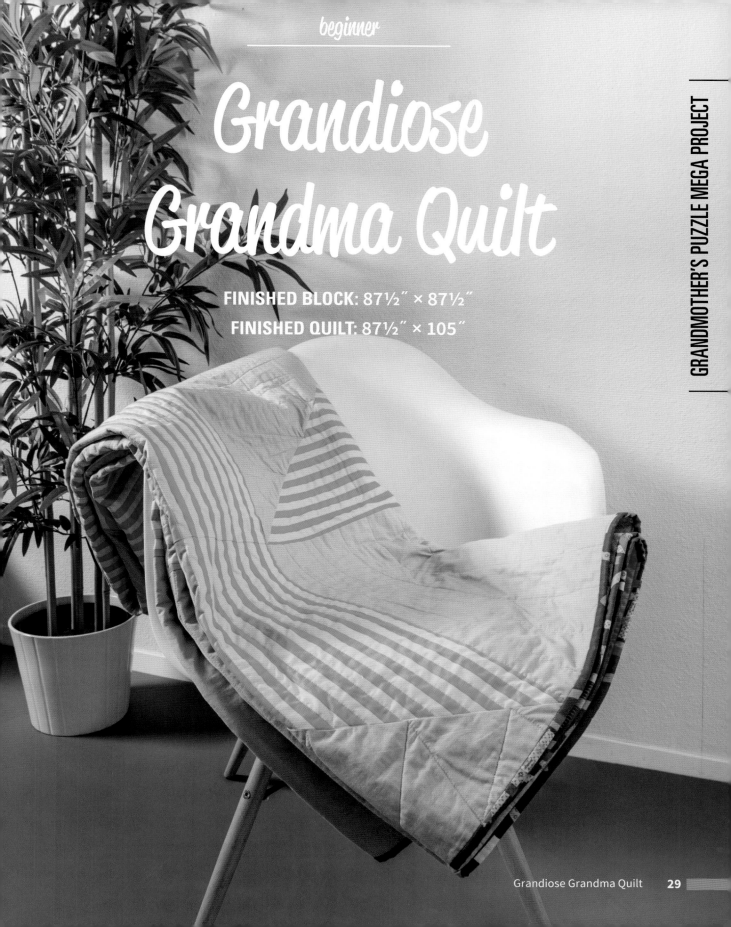

Grandiose Grandma Quilt

FINISHED BLOCK: 87½″ × 87½″

FINISHED QUILT: 87½″ × 105″

Skill Builders

Half-square triangles, 2-in-1 method	Large-scale construction
Fussy cutting	Quilt finishing

Get ready for a super-fast finished quilt top with a gigantic side of impact!

Materials

Please note that these fabric requirements leave no room for error. If you think you may need extra, buy an additional ¾ yard of each in order to get the required cuts. • Fabric requirements are based on 40˝ width of fabric unless otherwise noted.

Aqua stripe: 2¼ yards for block (If your fabric is directional, add more to accommodate.)

Coral: 1 yard for corners

Black text: 1 fat quarter for center

Gray: 3½ yards for background

Binding: ¾ yard

Backing: 108˝ wide, 2¾ yards

Batting: 96˝ × 113˝

Cutting

Aqua stripe

- Cut 2 strips 19˝ × width of fabric; subcut 4 squares 19˝ × 19˝.

- Cut 2 strips 18˝ × width of fabric; subcut 4 squares 18˝ × 18˝.

Coral: Cut 2 strips 18˝ × width of fabric; subcut 4 squares 18˝ × 18˝.

Black text: Cut 1 square 18˝ × 18˝. This is a fun spot to showcase a favorite fabric!

Gray

- Cut 2 strips 19˝ × width of fabric; subcut 4 squares 19˝ × 19˝.

- Cut 2 strips 18˝ × width of fabric; subcut 4 squares 18˝ × 18˝.

- Cut 5 strips 8¾˝ × width of fabric; cut 1 strip in half width-wise to make 2 half-strips.

Binding: Cut 10 strips 2½˝ × width of fabric.

Construction

Seam allowances are ¼″ unless otherwise noted.

Half-Square Triangles

1. Follow the instructions for Grandmother's Puzzle Block Construction (page 28), but use the 19″ squares in gray and aqua stripe to make 8 half-square triangles.

2. Square up the half-square triangles to 18″ × 18″.

Borders

1. Join 2½ gray strips together end to end with a straight seam. Trim the long strip to 88″ to make a top border. Repeat to make a bottom border.

2. Sew the borders to the top and bottom, pressing seam allowances toward the borders.

Finishing

Layer, quilt, and bind as desired. See *Quilt Finishing* (page 117).

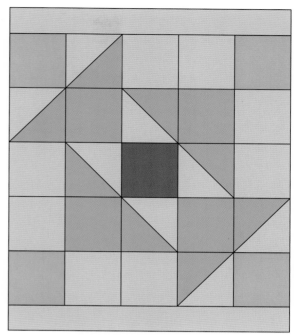

Quilt assembly

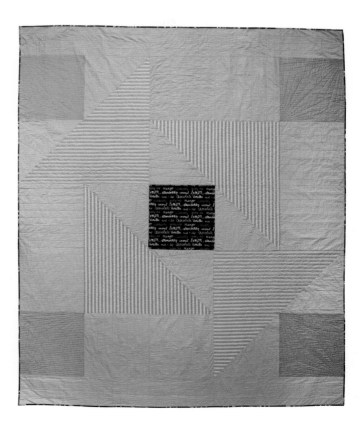

Granny Shams

FINISHED BLOCK: 10″ × 10″

FINISHED SHAM WITH FLANGE: 30″ × 22″

Skill Builders

Half-square triangles, 4-in-1 method

Overlap-close pillow construction

Creating a flanged edge

No need to be aSHAMed of your bed! By using parts of a block and mixing them in with a full block, you'll have the prettiest shams to be proud of!

Materials

These materials are for one sham only. Fabric requirements are based on 40˝ width of fabric unless otherwise noted. Fat quarters are 18˝ × 21˝; fat eighths are 9˝ × 21˝.

Aqua: ¾ yard for background and half-square triangles

Yellow: 1 fat quarter for block and side units

Pink: 1 fat eighth for corners and side units

Focus fabric: 1 scrap at least 2½˝ square for center

Pillow backing: 1½ yards

Batting: 30˝ × 22˝

Muslin: 30˝ × 22˝

Pillow form: 26˝ × 20˝

Cutting

Aqua

- Cut 3 strips 4½˝ × width of fabric.

  From 1 strip, subcut 2 rectangles 4½˝ × 10½˝ for block sashing and 4 squares 4½˝ × 4½˝ for half-square triangles.

  From 2 strips, subcut 10 squares 4½˝ × 4½˝ for half-square triangles and side units.

- Cut 4 strips 2½˝ × width of fabric.

  From 1 strip, subcut 8 squares 2½˝ × 2½˝ for blocks and 2 rectangles 2½˝ × 8½˝ for side unit sashing.

  From 1 strip, subcut 2 strips 2½˝ × 18˝ for flange.

  From 2 strips, trim to 2½˝ × 30˝ for flange.

Yellow

- Cut 2 strips 4½˝ × 21˝; subcut 6 squares 4½˝ × 4½˝ for half-square triangles.

- Cut 2 strips 2½˝ × 21˝; subcut 12 squares 2½˝ × 2½˝.

Pink: Cut 2 strips 2½˝ × 21˝; subcut 12 squares 2½˝ × 2½˝ for block corners.

Focus fabric: Cut 1 square 2½˝ × 2½˝ for center. This is a great size to fussy cut that perfect little design from a favorite print!

Pillow backing: Cut 2 rectangles 22˝ × 22½˝.

Construction

Seam allowances are ¼″ unless otherwise noted.

Half-Square Triangles

If you are worried about bias edges, you may want to starch the 4½″ squares and iron-dry them thoroughly before beginning this section.

1. Follow the instructions in Grandmother's Puzzle Block Construction (page 28), but use 6 yellow and 6 aqua 4½″ squares. This time make 24 *half-square triangles with the 4-in-1 method* (page 111).

2. Square up the half-square triangles to 2½″ × 2½″.

Side Unit Construction

1. With the remaining 2½″ squares and half-square triangles, make 8 four-patch units. Press the seam allowances away from the half-square triangles. **FIG. A**

2. Pair 2 four-patch units with 2 aqua 4½″ squares to create a larger four-patch unit. Make 2 variations as shown (**FIG. B**). Press the seam allowances away from the four-patch units.

3. Sew an aqua rectangle 2½″ × 8½″ between 2 variations of larger four-patch units to create a side unit (**FIG. C**). *Note the orientation of the blocks before sewing!* Press all the seams toward the aqua rectangle.

4. Repeat Steps 2 and 3 to make a second side unit.

Block Assembly

Using the following 2½″ squares make 1 block.

4 yellow

4 pink

1 focus

8 aqua

8 yellow/aqua half-square triangles

Pillow Top Assembly

1. Lay out the 10″ Grandmother's Puzzle block, 2 aqua rectangles 4½″ × 10½″, and 2 side units. **FIG. D**

2. Sew the aqua rectangles to the top and bottom of the Grandmother's Puzzle block.

3. Sew the side units to the Grandmother's Puzzle section, pressing the seams open.

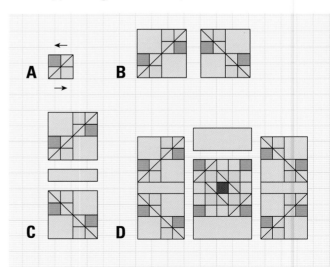

Pillow Assembly

1. Layer the pillow top face up on top of the batting and muslin rectangles and quilt as desired. See *Quilt Finishing* (page 117). Trim off the excess batting and muslin.

2. Attach the 18˝ flange strips to both sides of the pillow top. Press the seam allowances toward the flange. Attach the 30˝ flange strips to the top and bottom. Press the seam allowances toward the flange. FIG. E

3. Fold under ½˝ on one of the 22½˝ edges of a pillow backing rectangle and press. Fold under ½˝ again to enclose the raw edge, then press and *topstitch* (page 116) in place. Repeat for the other pillow backing rectangle.

4. Layer and pin in this order:

a. Pillow top, right side up

b. First pillow backing rectangle, right side down, hemmed edge in the center and raw edges lined up on the left edge

c. Second pillow backing rectangle, right side down, hemmed edge in the center and raw edges lined up on the right edge

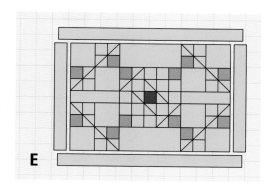

E

5. Sew around all 4 sides. *Clip the corners* (page 115), turn right side out, and press.

6. With the top of the pillow facing up, stitch-in-the-ditch in the seam where the flange meets the pillow top. This will encase the raw edges and create the flange.

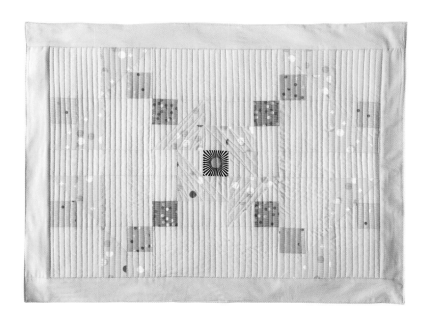

Stuff in a pillow, plump it up, and snuggle in!

Puzzling Patriarch Pillow

FINISHED BLOCK: 5″ × 5″
FINISHED PILLOW: 20″ × 20″

Skill Builders

Half-square triangles, 8-in-1 method

Sashings and cornerstones

Quilting

Inserting a piping edge

Overlap-close pillow construction

These pint-size blocks pack a huge punch when used in abundance!

Materials

Fabric requirements are based on 40″ width of fabric unless otherwise noted. Fat eighths are 9″ × 21″; fat quarters are 18″ × 21″.

Yellow: 1 fat quarter for blocks

Pink: 1 fat eighth for corners

Black: 1 charm square or scraps for centers

Pale aqua: ¾ yard for background

Pillow backing: ¾ yard

Batting: 22″ × 22″

Muslin: 22″ × 22″

Premade aqua piping: 2½ yards (or use 1 fat eighth and 2½ yards of ¼″ cording)

Pillow form: 21″ × 21″

Cutting

Yellow

- Cut 2 strips 4″ × 21″; subcut 9 squares 4″ × 4″ for half-square triangles.

- Cut 3 strips 1½″ × 21″; subcut 36 squares 1½″ × 1½″ for blocks.

Pink

- Cut 2 strips 1¾″ × 21″; subcut 16 squares 1¾″ × 1¾″ for cornerstones.

- Cut 3 strips 1½″ × 21″; subcut 36 squares 1½″ × 1½″ for block corners.

Black: Cut 9 squares 1½″ × 1½″ for block centers.

Pale aqua

- Cut 1 strip 4″ × width of fabric; subcut 9 squares 4″ × 4″ for half-square triangles.

- Cut 4 strips 1¾″ × width of fabric; subcut 24 rectangles 1¾″ × 5½″ for sashing.

- Cut 3 strips 1½″ × width of fabric; subcut 72 squares 1½″ × 1½″ for block background.

Piping (optional): Cut 5 strips 1¼″ × 21″.

Pillow backing: Cut 2 rectangles 16″ × 20″.

Construction

Seam allowances are ¼″ unless otherwise noted.

Half-Square Triangles

1. Follow the instructions in Grandmother's Puzzle Block Construction (page 28), but use 9 yellow and 9 pale aqua 4″ squares. This time make 72 *half-square triangles with the 8-in-1 method* (page 111).

2. Square up the half-square triangles to 1½″ × 1½″.

Block Assembly

1. Using the following 1½˝ squares make 1 block:

  4 yellow

  4 pink

  1 black

  8 pale aqua

  8 pale aqua/yellow half-square triangles

2. Repeat Step 1 another 8 more times for a total of 9 blocks.

Pillow Assembly

See the pressing arrows on the pillow assembly diagram.

1. Lay the 9 blocks in 3 rows of 3, inserting sashing rectangles and cornerstones as shown.

2. Sew the pieces together in rows, then sew the rows together.

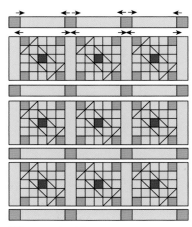

Pillow assembly

Finishing

1. Layer the pillow top face up on top of the batting and muslin squares. Quilt as desired. See *Quilt Finishing* (page 117). Trim off the excess batting and muslin.

2. Prepare your *piping* (page 116) if you are making your own. Starting at the bottom center, pin the piping around all 4 sides of the pillow top, aligning raw edges of the piping and pillow. Make gentle curves at each corner, and leave a little tail at the beginning and end. Make a clip into the piping seam allowance at each corner to help ease the piping around the corner.

4. Baste with an ⅛˝ seam allowance.

5. Press under ½˝ on one 16˝ edge of a pillow backing rectangle. Press under ½˝ again to enclose the raw edge, then *topstitch* (page 116) in place. Repeat for the other pillow backing rectangle.

6. Layer and pin in this order:

  a. Pillow top, right side up

  b. Pillow backing rectangle, right side down, hemmed edge in the center and raw edges lined up on the top edge

  c. Second pillow backing rectangle, right side down, hemmed edge in the center and raw edges lined up on the bottom edge

7. Using a zipper foot and with the needle in the leftmost position, sew around all 4 sides with the edge of the zipper foot tight against the piping. Clip the corners and overlock the edges, or zigzag all edges to keep things tidy. Turn right side out and press.

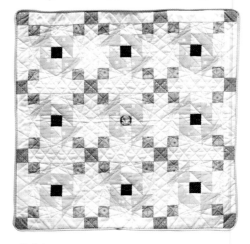

8. Insert the pillow form. I like to use a pillow form that's slightly larger than the pillow cover. The pillow size listed in Materials (page 37) will give this pillow a nice plump finish.

3

Irish Logs

Catch that spill!

For those of you out there who don't have children, know that eating is extremely hard to do when you're six and eight (rolls eyes). Pick up food, insert into mouth, chew, swallow, and repeat. But in between all of those steps, spill the food on the table. Okay, I may be exaggerating a touch. (*Ahem.*) So while place mats might save me from scraping porridge off the table, some days I just feel it would be easier to roll out a table runner as a place mat and save myself from the horror that is grade-school food-fight-style messes on my table.

IRISH LOGS BLOCK   40

Mega Project
Run, Run, Runner   43

Medium Project
Hidden-Agenda Pocket
Place Mat   45

Micro Project
Positively Petite Coasters   50

IRISH LOGS BLOCK

The Irish Logs block is a fun blend of an Irish Chain and a Log Cabin that can have some serious impact with fussy-cut directional prints! I adore this block and its mad number of pieces, especially when it goes micro, swoon! I'm already dreaming of a full quilt in this block!

Block Essentials

This is what is needed to make the sample block. All individual sizes are included with the actual projects.

Block sashing:
12 large rectangles

Center nine-patch:
9 squares

Corner squares:

• *Side wings A and B:*

  16 small rectangles

  8 squares for corner-square triangles

• *Half-square triangles:* 2 squares for 4 half-square triangles

• *Large four-patch:* 12 large squares

• *Small four-patch:* 16 small squares

Skill Builders

Half-square triangles, 2-in-1 method

Corner-square triangles

Irish Logs Block Construction

The following instructions are for a single Irish Logs block. Seam allowances are ¼″ unless otherwise noted. Press all the seams open unless otherwise noted.

The Irish Logs block is made up of 3 elements, a center nine-patch, block sashing, and corner squares. Each corner square has 4 parts—a large four-patch which includes a half-square triangle, a small four-patch and 2 side wings A and B. Once all the components are complete, the block is sewn together much like a nine-patch.

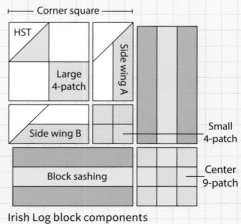

Irish Log block components

Center Nine-Patch

Using 9 squares—4 of one color and 5 of another color (or substitute 4 of a second color and 1 fussy-cut square for the center)—make a *nine-patch unit* (page 112).

Block Sashing

1. Select 3 block sashing rectangles—2 in one color and a 1 in a different color.

2. Sew the 2 rectangles of the same color to each side of the third rectangle lengthwise. Make 4.

Corner Squares

Half-Square Triangles

1. Pair 2 different color squares right sides together. Repeat for a second pair.

2. Make 4 *half-square triangles using the 2-in-1 method* (page 111).

3. Square up to the same size as the large four-patch squares.

Large Four-Patch

1. Lay out 1 half-square triangle and 3 of the large four-patch squares in the colors needed for your project to make a large *four-patch unit* (page 112) as shown.

2. Repeat Step 1 to make 4 large four-patch units.

Small Four-Patch

1. Using 4 of the small four-patch squares—2 of one color and 2 of another color—make a small four-patch unit as shown.

2. Repeat Step 1 to make 4 small four-patch units.

Side Wings A and B

1. Select 2 side wing rectangles—one each of 2 colors. Sew them together lengthwise to make a side wing segment. Repeat to make 8 segments.

2. Following the image of side wing A, use 4 of the side wing squares to sew **corner-square triangles** (page 111) to one end of 4 side wing A segments. Pay close attention to *the color orientation of each side wing segment,* and to *the angle of the corner-square triangle.* Refer to your project image for the correct color placement.

3. Repeat Step 2 using the other 4 segments to make 4 side wing B units.

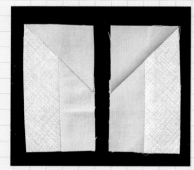

Side wings A and B

Corner Square Assembly

1. For each corner square lay out 1 large and 1 small four-patch, 1 side wing A, and 1 side wing B as shown in the image below.

2. Double check the orientation of each block element before sewing the blocks together as you would a four-patch unit.

3. Repeat Steps 1 and 2 another 3 times to make 4 corner squares.

Irish Logs Block Assembly

1. Arrange the center nine-patch, 4 corner squares, and 4 block sashing units as shown. Make sure the half-square triangle of each corner square is on the outside corner, and that the same color squares of the four- and nine-patches line up on the block's 2 diagonals.

2. Sew the block units together as if they were a part of a nine-patch block.

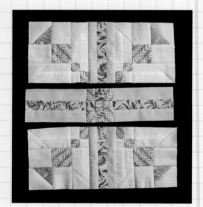

Run, Run, Runner

FINISHED BLOCK: 20⅛″ × 20⅛″

FINISHED TABLE RUNNER: 20⅛″ × 60⅜″

Skill Builders

Quilt finishing

These large-scale blocks look fantastic in a set of three as a table runner, but can you imagine them together as a quilt?! Someone needs to get on that stat!

Materials

Fabric requirements are based on 40″ width of fabric unless otherwise noted. Fat quarters are 18″ × 21″.

Aqua: ⅓ yard for corner squares and center nine-patch units

Light pink: ⅜ yard for corner squares

Pink: ⅜ yard for block sashing

Yellow: 1 fat quarter for block sashing and center nine-patch units

White tonal: ¾ yard for corner squares

Binding: ⅓ yard

Backing: 1½ yards

Batting: 28″ × 68″

Cutting

FOR	CUT	QUANTITY				
		Aqua	**Light pink**	**Pink**	**Yellow**	**White tonal**
Center nine-patch	1⅞″ square	15			12	
Block sashing	1⅞″ × 8½″ rectangle			24	12	
Corner squares:						
Half-square triangle	3¾″ square	6				6
Large four-patch	3⅛″ square	12				24
Small four-patch	1⅞″ square	24	24			
	1⅞″ × 5¾″ rectangle		24			24
Side wings	3¼″ square for corner-square triangle					24

Block Construction

Seam allowances are ¼″ unless otherwise noted.

1. Follow the instructions in Irish Logs Block Construction (page 40); repeat 3 times to make 3 mega blocks.

2. Sew the 3 blocks together in a row.

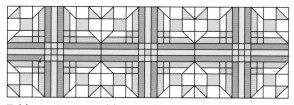

Table runner assembly

Finishing

Layer, quilt as desired and bind. See *Quilt Finishing* (page 117).

Hidden-Agenda Pocket Place Mat

FINISHED BLOCK: 9⅝″ × 9⅝″

FINISHED PLACE MAT: 17⅝″ × 13⅝″

┌─────────────────────────┐
│ ## Skill Builders   │
│   │
│ Making a simple pocket │
│   │
│ Quilt finishing   │
└─────────────────────────┘

The perfect place mat to either help your child set the table (just insert cutlery into the pocket and you're ready to go!) or help your child hide his broccoli (just insert broccoli and you're ready to go!).

Materials

These materials are for one place mat. Fabric requirements are based on 40″ width of fabric unless otherwise noted. Fat quarters are 18″ × 21″; fat eighths are 9″ × 21″; charm squares are 5″ × 5″.

Aqua: ⅔ yard corner squares, place mat borders, pocket, and binding

Yellow: 1 fat quarter for large four-patches, small four-patches, and center nine-patch

Textured gray: 1 fat quarter for side wings

Solid gray: 1 fat eighth for block and border sashing

Pink: 1 fat eighth for block and border sashing

Coral (optional): 1 charm square for center nine-patch and half-square triangles

Backing: 1 fat quarter

Batting: 1 rectangle 18″ × 20″

Cutting

FOR	CUT	QUANTITY					
		Aqua	**Yellow**	**Textured gray**	**Solid gray**	**Pink**	**Coral (optional)**
Center nine-patch	1⅛″ square		5			4	1*
Block sashing	1⅛″ × 4½″ rectangle				8	4	
Corner squares:							
Half-square triangle	2⅜″ square	2	2				2*
Large four-patch	1⅞″ square	8	4				
Small four-patch	1⅛″ square		8	8			
Side wings	1⅛″ × 3¼″ rectangle	8		8			
	1¾″ square for corner-square triangle	8					
Place mat borders and pocket	4½″ × 6⅜″ rectangle	6					
	2½″ × 4⅜″ rectangle	4					
Border sashing	4½″ × 1⅛″ rectangle				4	2	
	2½″ × 1⅛″ rectangle				4	2	
Binding	2″ × width of fabric strip	2					

* Use this print as a substitute for the nine-patch center square and the squares used to make the half-square triangles; otherwise, use the yellow fabric indicated.

Construction

Seam allowances are ¼″ unless otherwise noted.

Follow the instructions in Irish Logs Block Construction (page 40) to make 1 medium block.

Borders

Use the cut strips indicated for the border.

1. Make border sashing by sewing 1 pink rectangle 2½″ × 1⅛″ between 2 solid gray rectangles of the same size lengthwise together. Make 2 border sashing segments.

2. Sew 2 aqua rectangles 2½″ × 4⅜″ to either side of a 2½″ border sashing segment to make the top border.

3. Repeat Step 2 for the bottom border.

4. Repeat Steps 1–3, but this time use the longer rectangles 4½″ × 1⅛″ for border sashing segments, and add the larger aqua rectangles 4½″ × 6⅜″ to make 2 side borders.

Place Mat Assembly

1. Add the top and bottom borders to the Irish Logs block, matching the strip set section to the block's sashing. Press toward the border.

2. Add the side borders to the Irish Logs block, matching the strip set section to the block's sashing. Press toward the border. FIG. A

Pocket and Finishing

1. Place the remaining 2 aqua rectangles 4½″ × 6⅜″ right sides together. Sew across the top (4½″-wide edge) and down the left side. *Clip the corner* (page 115) and turn right side out and press.

2. Topstitch across the top. Set aside for the pocket, to be added after quilting the place mat.

3. Layer and quilt as desired. See *Quilt Finishing* (page 117).

4. Place the pocket right side up on the bottom right corner of the place mat, aligning raw edges. Baste the right side and bottom edge in place.

5. *Topstitch* (page 116) down the left side of the pocket, backstitching in the top left corner. FIG. B

3. Bind as desired. See Quilt Finishing (page 117).

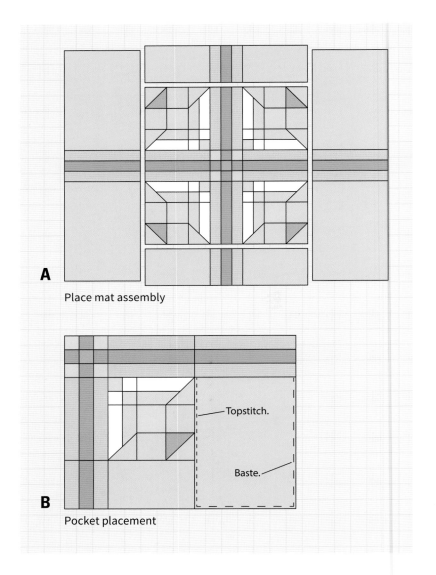

A

Place mat assembly

B

Pocket placement

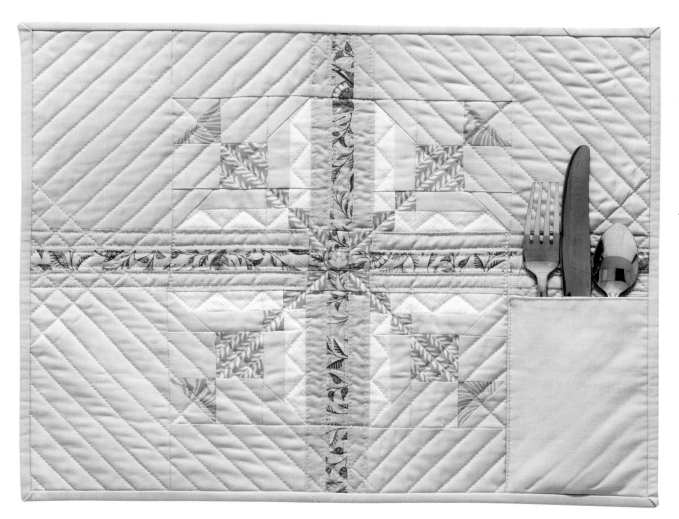

Positively Petite Coasters

FINISHED COASTER: 5⅛″ × 5⅛″

Skill Builders

Half-square triangles, 2-in-1 method

Corner square triangles

Small-scale piecing

Quilt finishing

While I love a good giant block, and traditionally sized blocks are what I work with most often, micro-pieced blocks have my heart. Something about working on such a small scale gets my quilty engine running! And what better way to showcase positively petite blocks? Well, with coasters, of course!

Materials

These materials are for 4 coasters. Fat quarters are 18″ × 21″; fat eighths are 9″ × 21″.

Pink: 1 fat eighth for large four-patch units, small four-patch units, and center nine-patch unit

Aqua: 1 fat eighth for block sashing and center nine-patch unit

Yellow: 1 fat eighth for block sashing

Textured gray: 1 fat quarter for corner squares

Light aqua/white print: 1 fat eighth for corner squares

Petite print (optional): Scraps for fussy-cut centers of center nine-patch unit

Backing: 1 fat quarter

Batting: 4 squares 9″ × 9″

Cutting

FOR	CUT	QUANTITY					
		Pink	Aqua	Yellow	Textured gray	Light aqua / White print	Petite print
Center nine-patch	⅞″ square	20	16				4*
Block sashing	⅞″ × 2½″ rectangle		16	32			
Corner squares:							
Half-square triangle	1¾″ square	8			8		
Large four-patch	1⅛″ square	16			32		
Small four-patch	⅞″ square	32				32	
	⅞″ × 1¾″ rectangle				32	32	
Side wings	1¼″ square for corner-square triangle				32		
Backing	4 squares 9″ × 9″						

Fussy-cut this print to substitute for 4 of the nine-patch center squares; otherwise cut pink squares for the centers.

Construction

Seam allowances are ¼˝ unless otherwise noted.

Follow the instructions in Irish Logs Block Construction (page 40); repeat 4 times to make 4 micro blocks.

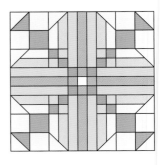

Finishing

1. Layer the top and batting (no backing) and quilt as desired. See **Quilt Finishing** (page 117).

2. Layer the backing fabric and the quilted coaster right sides together. Lockstitching at the start and end, sew around all 4 sides, leaving a 2½˝–3˝ opening on one side for turning. Clip corners making sure not to cut into the seam allowance.

3. Turn right side out. Push out the corners with a chopstick and press.

4. Turn the raw edges of the opening to the inside and pin closed. Topstitch around the entire coaster close to the edge, making sure to lockstitch at the start and end.

TIP

Don't need 4 coasters? Maybe just one with a great mug and some specialty teas for a teacher gift? Just substitute fat eighths for fat quarters and 10˝ squares for fat eighths and divide the cutting instructions by four—and there you have it! Exactly what you need to make one positively perfect coaster.

4

Dresden Plate

Double, double ... no toil, no trouble!

Dresdens are my favorite—all time, ever and forever, and ever. But not regular Dresdens, I mean they're pretty great too, but my favorite Dresdens are what I like to call double-ended Star Dresdens, where you make a point at each end of the Dresden Plate wedge. I love them so much that right now, I currently have four Star Dresden projects on the go, three of which are quilts!

DRESDEN PLATE BLOCK 54

Mega Project
By Day and by Night Quilt 56

Medium Project
Two-Face Pillowcase 61

Micro Project
Lash-Lovely Sleep Mask 65

DRESDEN PLATE BLOCK

The Dresden Plate block, in its simplicity, has the ability to transform into some of the most amazing quilts. And with the plate being appliquéd onto the background fabric, smaller versions of it are perfect for hand appliqué and work great as a travel project!

Block Essentials

This is what is needed to make the sample block. All individual sizes are included with the actual projects.

Assorted strips: 36 assorted strips to make one full circle

Fabric glue: For glue basting (I like Roxanne Glue-Baste-It.)

Paper, card stock, or template plastic: To make a template

Dresden Plate Block Construction

Seam allowances are ¼″ unless otherwise noted. Press all the seams open unless otherwise noted.

Preparation

Use the Dresden Plate patterns (pullout page P1). For more information about creating a template, refer to Handy Tips, Techniques, and Terminology, **Making a Template** *(page 117).*

1. Make a paper template from the appropriate Dresden pattern.

2. To cut the Dresden wedges, stack up to 4 layers of fabric at a time. Place the wide end of the template parallel to the selvage or, align the template with the top and bottom of a strip that has been cut to size. Lay a ruler over top of the template, aligning the ruler edge to the template edge. Cut, sliding the ruler along the template edge if the wedge is longer than the ruler.

3. Repeat on the opposite side of the wedge. **FIG. A**

TIP

Try stacking some fabrics together to cut several at once. I like to stack 4 strips before cutting. It helps to place a piece of rolled up tape on the back of the template to keep it from shifting off the fabric!

A

Dresden Wedge

1. Fold the Dresden wedge in half lengthwise, right sides together, and sew across both the bottom edge and the top edge. While the wedge is still folded, gently finger-press a crease to mark the center of each end. **FIG. B**

B

TIP

Chain piecing (page 115) can really speed up the process. If the pieces are long enough, the top and bottom can be chain pieced together, which saves even more time! Try sewing the wide end of the wedge first, then bring the narrow end up and continue sewing.

2. Finger-press the seams open and turn the wedge right side out. Gently push the points out. Align the seams with the center crease and press. Repeat with all wedges. **FIG. C**

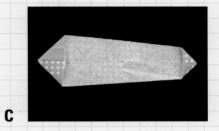

C

Block Assembly

1. Arrange the wedges in your desired layout. Sew together in pairs side-to-side starting at the wide end and *lockstitching* (page 116) at the start and end. **FIG. D**

2. Sew pairs together to form the Dresden Plate. The Dresden Plate is now ready to be sewn onto the background! **FIG. E**

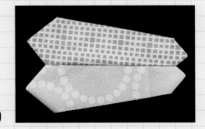

D

3. The Dresden Plate is appliquéd to the background. I like to *glue baste* (page 112) instead of pinning. Use tiny dots of glue under each of the points, top and bottom. If you are new to appliqué, try this easy-to-stitch method. Just turn under any raw edges of the appliqué piece ¼″ that will not be enclosed in a seam, and place the piece on the background. *Topstitch* (page 116) close to the edge all the way around the appliqué.

E

By Day and by Night Quilt

FINISHED BLOCK: 34½″ × 66½″

FINISHED QUILT: 70″ × 90″

Skill Builders

Stack-cutting Dresden Plate wedges

Making Dresden Plate wedges

Large-scale block construction

Easy straight-stitch machine appliqué

Making a double-sided quilt

Quilt finishing

Giant Dresdens are the perfect project when you need a powerful impact without a lot of effort. We all need a project like that once in a while, right? This one's made with two half-Dresden plates to make a double-sided quilt, because double-sided quilts are twice the fun, especially for quilt forts!

Materials

Fabric requirements are based on 40˝ width of fabric unless otherwise noted.

Assorted warms: ¼ yard of 19 various fabrics

Assorted cools: ¼ yard of 19 various fabrics

Binding: ½ yard

Background fabric: 2 yards 108˝-wide *each* in white for Day, black for Night

Batting: 76˝ × 108˝

Other supplies

Fabric glue: To secure appliqué

Spray adhesive: For quilt sandwich

Paper: To make a template

Cutting

Assorted warms and cools: From *each* ¼ yard, cut 1 rectangle 6½˝ × 27˝.

Binding: Cut 6 strips 2˝ × width of fabric.

Note | *You can easily cut a Mega Dresden wedge from a 27˝ strip of fabric. But what if you want to use what you have on hand and you're more of a fat-quarter kind of hoarder … errr, curator? Easy solution—piece some extra strips into your fat quarter before cutting the wedges! This also gives you an opportunity to add in little fussy cuts or break up a solid with a pop of print.*

Construction

Seam allowances are ¼˝ unless otherwise noted.

Assembly

Use the Mega Dresden Plate pattern (pullout page P1).

1. Follow the instructions in Dresden Plate Block Construction (page 54).

2. From assorted warm and cool rectangles, cut 19 Dresden wedges from each group.

3. Make a half-Dresden Plate with the 19 warm colors and another half-Dresden Plate with the 19 cool colors.

Appliqué

1. Fold the white Day background in half horizontally and lightly press a line.

2. With the right side face up, place the warm Dresden Plate, right side up, so the middle wedge sits on the line. It doesn't need to line up perfectly, it just needs to be close.

3. Move the Dresden Plate toward the right edge until the points on the small end of the Dresden wedges are ¼˝ from the edge of the background fabric. The wide ends of the wedges will overhang the edge. Pin in place. **FIG.A**

4. *Glue baste* (page 112) all the points with *fabric glue* (page 120) on the Dresden Plate and machine appliqué. I like to just *topstitch* (page 116) as close to the appliqué edge as possible for this. But you could choose to use a decorative stitch for some added interest! Remove the pins and trim the wedges even with the quilt top.

5. Repeat Steps 1–4 with the cool Dresden Plate on the black Night background, but instead align the Dresden plate to the left side.

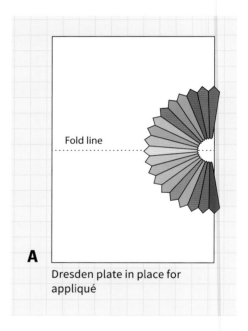

Fold line

A

Dresden plate in place for appliqué

TIP

I use my zipper foot for appliqué. I like that I can adjust my needle all the way over and use the edge of the zipper foot as my guide!

Finishing

Finishing this quilt is a little different than most, but it works out fine in the end! Refer to **Quilt Finishing** (page 117) to see how things are normally done.

1. Lay the batting out flat. Place the warm Day side face up on the batting, lining up the right edge of the background with the right edge of the batting.

2. **Spray baste** (page 112) the quilt to the batting.

3. Place the cool Night side face down on top of the warm Day side, lining up the Dresden Plate again on the right side. Don't be overly concerned if your Dresdens don't match up perfectly; they will be on opposite sides of the quilt and you will never actually see them together! Pin along the Dresden edge.

4. With a ¼˝ seam allowance, sew everything together along the right side.

5. Flip the cool Night side over to the back of the quilt. The cool Night side is now face up on the batting.

6. Lay the quilt warm Day side down and spray baste the cool Night side in place.

7. Quilt as desired, but read the tip first!

> ### TIP
> Treat the sewn edge as an already bound side, meaning if you want to quilt off the edge as you normally would, take care when doing so. The edge is already finished and you won't be squaring it up, so be careful of the fabric pushing!

Double-Fold Binding

1. Square up the 3 unfinished sides and trim the quilt to 70˝ × 90˝.

2. Prepare the 2˝ *double-fold binding* (page 114).

3. Fold one end of the binding under ½˝. Start binding at the bottom right corner with the binding overhanging the edge of the quilt ⅛˝.

4. *Lockstitch* (page 116) and sew the binding around the 3 unfinished sides, stopping a few inches from the edge of the quilt and lockstitching again. Trim the excess binding at the end, leaving a ⅝˝ tail past the edge of the quilt. Fold the binding end under ½˝ and finish sewing in place, lockstitching at the start and finish.

5. Fold the binding over to the back and hand stitch down; hand stitch the 2 binding ends closed. FIG. B

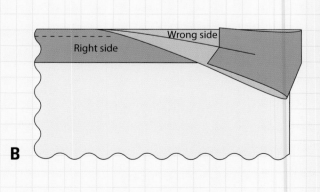

Right side

Wrong side

B

Two-Face Pillowcase

FINISHED BLOCK: 12″ × 12″

FINISHED PILLOWCASE: 21″ × 30″

Skill Builders

Stack-cutting Dresden Plate wedges

Making Dresden Plate wedges

Easy straight-stitch machine appliqué

Pillowcase construction

French seams

Night side or Day side, the Two-Face Pillowcase has you covered on style! And with two pretty sides, it has you covered on accidental drooling as well.

Materials

These materials are for 1 pillowcase. Fabric requirements are based on 40˝ width of fabric unless otherwise noted.

Assorted warms: 9 scraps minimum 3˝ × 8˝

Assorted cools: 9 scraps minimum 3˝ × 8˝

Main body: ¾ yard *each* in light (for warm side) and dark (for cool side) fabrics

Trim: 2 strips minimum 2˝ × 23˝: 1 for warm side, 1 for cool side

Cuff: ¼ yard *each* of 2 fabrics: 1 for warm side, 1 for cool side

Other supplies

Water-soluble pen

Basting glue

Paper: To make a template

Cutting

Assorted warms and cools: Trim all scraps to 3˝ × 8˝ rectangles; make 18 total.

Main body: Cut 2 rectangles 23˝ × 27˝: 1 light, 1 dark.

Trim: Cut 2 strips 2˝ × 23˝: 1 for warm side, 1 for cool side.

Cuff: *Carefully* cut 2 strips 9˝ × 23˝: 1 for warm side, 1 for cool side.

Construction

Seam allowances are ¼˝ unless otherwise noted.

Pillow Assembly

Use the Medium Dresden Plate pattern (pullout page P1).

1. Follow the instructions in Dresden Plate Block Construction (page 54).

2. From assorted warm and assorted cool rectangles, cut 9 Dresden wedges for *each* group.

3. Make a partial plate using 9 wedges in warm fabrics. Make a second partial plate using 9 wedges in cool fabrics.

Adding the Trim and Cuff

1. Press the warm trim strip in half lengthwise, wrong sides together.

2. With the warm cuff face up, long edges to the left and right, place the trim along the 23″ left side, matching the raw edges. Pin in place. FIG. A

3. Place the light main body 23″ edge right sides together along the left edge, on top of the cuff and the trim. Re-pin all layers together along the left edge. Roll the body fabric up so it sits in the middle between the left and right edges of the cuff. FIG. B

4. Wrap the right edge of the cuff over the rolled body fabric and line it up with the left edge as well. Re-pin all the layers and sew the left edge with a ¼″ seam. It should look like a fabric-stuffed burrito.

5. Pull the fabric carefully out one end of the pillowcase burrito so the cuff turns right side out. Press. FIG. C

6. Repeat Steps 1–5 with the dark main body, and the cool side trim and cuff fabrics.

Dresden Plate Appliqué

1. Orient the light main body side face up with the cuff on the left side. Mark the centerline from the bottom right corner. To do this, align the 45° line on a ruler with the bottom edge of the fabric and match the edge of the ruler to the corner of the fabric. With a water-soluble pen, draw about a 10″ centerline starting about 5″ out from the corner. FIG. D

2. Now mark 2 more lines. First draw a 4″ vertical line, ½″ in from the right edge and about 5″ up from the bottom corner. Repeat for another

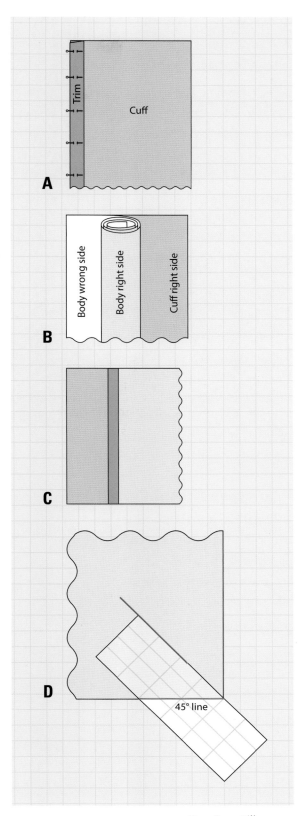

4″ line, this time horizontal, 5″ from the corner and ½″ up from the bottom edge. You now have side and bottom lines marked. **FIG. E**

3. With the right side up, place the warm partial Dresden Plate so the points of the center wedge align with the centerline. Shift the Dresden up or down the centerline until the small end of the outermost Dresden wedges line up somewhere along the side and bottom lines. As long as the center wedge is on the centerline and the small ends of the outermost wedges touch the side and bottom lines, it is in the right spot. **FIG. F**

4. *Glue baste* (page 112) the Dresden Plate points in place. Machine appliqué by topstitching the Dresden Plate to the background.

5. Repeat Steps 1–4 with the dark main body, and cool partial Dresden, this time making sure to orient the cuff on the right side and marking the centerline from the bottom left corner. The cool Dresden Plate is appliquéd to the left side of the main body fabric.

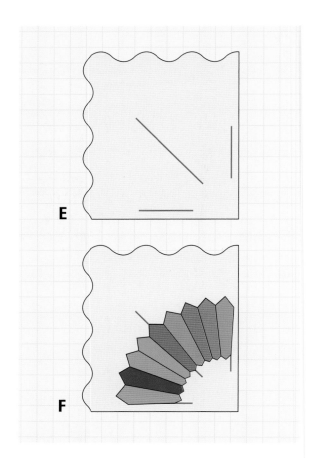

E

F

Pillowcase Assembly

1. Place both main body pieces *wrong sides together* with cuff and trim lined up. Sew all 3 raw sides with a scant ¼″ seam allowance. Clip corners.

2. Turn right sides in, press, and sew all 3 sides with a ½″ seam allowance, to make a French seam.

3. Turn right side out again and press to complete the pillowcase.

Lash-Lovely Sleep Mask

FINISHED BLOCK: 3¼″ × 1¼″
FINISHED MASK: 7″ × 3¼″

Skill Builders

Making Dresden Plate wedges

Fussy cutting (optional)

Easy straight-stitch machine appliqué

Quilting

Mask construction

I just couldn't resist fussy cutting the print for this project to look like long lashes, (with some seriously crazy eye shadow!). It was one of those things where as soon as the idea popped into my head, it needed to happen! Have fun playing with prints to see what you can come up with!

Materials

Fabric requirements are based on 40˝ width of fabric unless otherwise noted.

Scraps: 10 scraps minimum 1¾˝ × 1¾˝

Mask front: 1 rectangle 4½˝ × 8½˝

Flannel back: 1 rectangle 4½˝ × 8½˝

Muslin: 2 rectangles 1¼˝ × 4˝

Batting: 1 rectangle 4½˝ × 8½˝

Other supplies

Elastic: ½˝ wide, 16˝ length

Paper or card stock: To make templates

Cutting

Scraps: From each scrap, cut 1 square 1¾˝ × 1¾˝.

Construction

Seam allowances are ¼˝ unless otherwise noted.

Dresden Plate Assembly

Use the Micro Dresden Plate pattern (pullout page P1) and the Sleep Mask pattern (pullout page P1).

1. Follow the instructions for Dresden Plate Block Construction (page 54).

2. Cut 10 Micro Dresden Plates from the 1¾˝ squares.

TIP

For the micro wedges, I fussy-cut the Clear Skies print from the Slow and Steady collection by Tula Pink for FreeSpirit Fabric. This fabric may or may not be available when you make your sleep mask, but look for lashes in unexpected places!

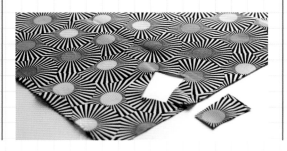

3. Sew points only at the wide end of the wedges. Leave the narrow ends unsewn. Make 2 Dresden Plate arcs, 5 wedges each.

4. Place a Dresden Plate unit right side down on a muslin rectangle. Starting just below the foldover from the point, *lockstitch* (page 116) and sew around the sides and bottom of the Dresden unit, stopping just before reaching the foldover. FIG. A

5. Turn the plate over and trim back the muslin so none of it overhangs the Dresden unit. Clip the corners. FIG. B

6. Turn right side out and gently push out the corners. FIG. C

Making the Mask

1. Create a *template* (page 117) of the Sleep Mask pattern, transferring the marks at both sides onto the template.

2. Baste the mask front rectangle onto the batting and quilt if desired. See *Quilt Finishing* (page 117).

3. Trim using the mask template and mark the side elastic placement.

4. Lay the Dresden lashes right side up on the mask front, moving them around until they look centered.

5. *Glue baste* (page 112) the points and a few spots along the top edge. Machine appliqué in place by *topstitching* (page 116). FIG. D

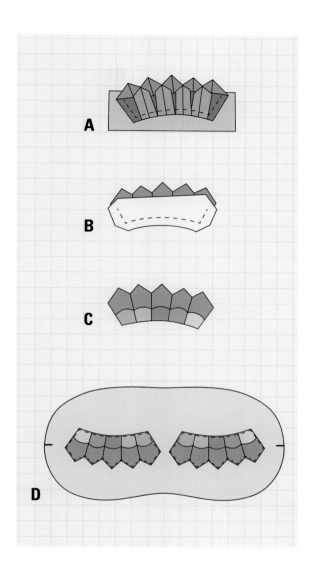

6. Center the ends of the elastic over the placement marks on each side. Be careful not to twist the elastic. Secure the ends in place with a *bar tack* (page 116) (a narrow zigzag stitch) keeping the stitches within the ¼˝ seam allowance. FIG.E

7. Cut a backing for the sleep mask from the flannel using the template.

8. Place the backing flannel face down on the mask front. Fold up the elastic and place a pin in it to help keep it out of the way. Sew around the perimeter, leaving a 2˝ gap for turning, and lockstitching at the start and end. FIG.F

9. Overcast edges if desired and turn right side out.

10. Close up the gap with a few pins and topstitch around the perimeter.

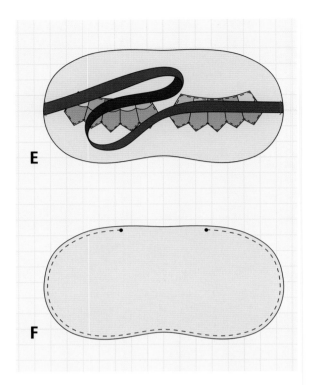

E

F

Now slide it on and have a nap!

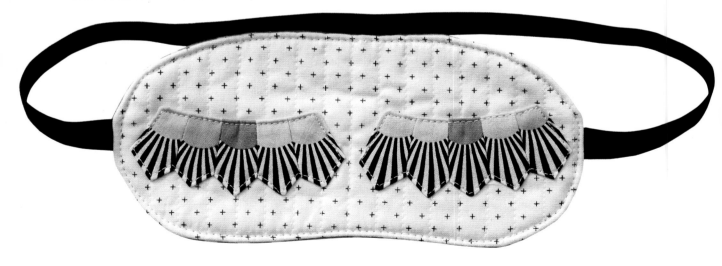

5

Hexagons

Hexies! And homework! Hooray!!

Wait what? Homework? That's right, homework. This trifecta of hexie awesomeness came about to help out my two little guys keep their school supplies easily available and give them a spot of their own to kick back and work out some tricky math equations. Okay, okay, I totally made all these things for me. But they would work for the kids, too.

HEXAGON BLOCK   70

Mega Project

Helloooo Hexie!
Floor Pillow   74

Medium Project

Snap-Flap
Notebook Cover   78

Micro Project

Flat-Pack
Pencil Case   85

HEXAGON BLOCK

Hand sewing hexies English Paper Piecing style, or EPP, can be a fun project to take with you on road trips, to the doctor's office, school pick-up, pretty much anywhere. Because of this, it's a popular way to sew hexies. Machine sewing them, however, is slightly less popular. It's the Y-seams isn't it? People are afraid of Y-seams. I'm here to show you that there's no reason to fear machine sewing hexies! It's easy!

Block Essentials

This is what is needed to make the sample block. All individual sizes are included with the actual projects.

Fabric: For hexagons

For English paper piecing:

English paper-piecing papers: See the size indicated on the pattern.

Glue stick/pen

Needles: I use John James milliners #10.

Thread: I use InvisaFil (by Wonderfil Specialty Threads).

For machine piecing:

Water-soluble pen

Ruler

Paper, card stock, or template plastic: For making a template

Thread: Such as Aurifil 50-weight

Hexagon Block Construction

Seam allowances are ¼˝ unless otherwise noted.

Preparation

If you want to make your own templates, use the Mega, Medium and Micro Hexagon patterns (pullout page P1). For more information about creating a template, refer to Handy Tips, Techniques, and Terminology, Making a Template (page 117).

English Paper Piecing

1. Using the English paper-piecing paper as a template, cut around the hexie with a rotary cutter and an acrylic ruler, adding a ¼˝ seam allowance on all sides. Alternatively, you can trace the hexagon paper or pattern onto template plastic and cut it out with a ¼˝ seam allowance.

2. Lay the fabric hexie right side down and center the paper hexie on top. Dab a little dot of glue and fold the fabric edge over the paper. Continue working around each side, being careful not to stretch the fabric around too tight. Stretching could warp the shape and make it hard to sew. FIG. A

3. Thread the needle—no knot, no doubling the thread, just a single strand.

4. Lay out the hexies in the order they are to be sewn. Choose 2 and place them right sides together with all sides lined up evenly.

5. Start at a corner and slide the needle in just under the fold, passing through both hexies. Don't pull all the way through; leave a little tail. Come over the top of the edge and slide the needle back into the same spot, leaving a loop on top. Pass the needle through the loop twice, and pull tight to make a knot. FIGS. B-E

TIP

I find tracing the hexies onto the fabric with a template and then cutting with scissors to be faster than having to reposition the ruler to cut each side with a rotary cutter. But find what works best for you and go with it!

A

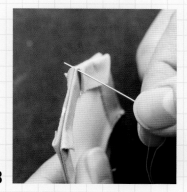

B

C

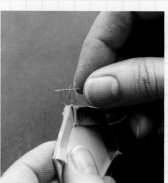

D

E

6. Whipstitch the length of the edge by sliding the needle in and catching just the tiniest amount of fabric on both hexies. Come up over the top of the edge and back through again, with stitches that are about ⅛″ apart. Be careful not to catch the papers. At the end of the edge, tie another knot as in Step 5. FIG.F

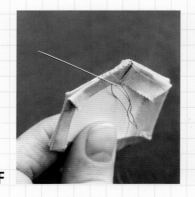

F

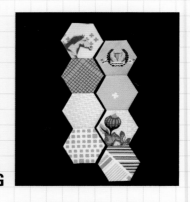

G

7. Sew all the hexies into rows. FIG.G

8. Sew the rows together by whipstitching down the zigzag. Flip 1 row of hexies over so 2 rows are right sides together and the first edges to be sewn are aligned. Continue to fold the hexies gently to sew down the zigzag, tying a knot at the end of every hexie. FIGS.H-I

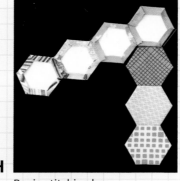

H

Begin stitching here.

I

Machine Piecing

1. Cut out all fabrics with a template made from the pattern. The seam allowance is already included in the Mega Hexagon pattern (pullout page P1).

2. On the wrong side of every hexie, mark the ¼″ seam allowance at the corners. A simple line at each corner all the way around will form small X's. The center of the X is where to start and stop sewing. FIG.J

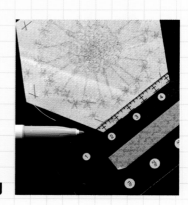

J

3. Line up 2 hexies right sides together. Drop the sewing machine needle in exactly at the X point. Lockstitch at the mark and continue sewing until the next mark, then lockstitch again. FIG. K

4. Sew all the hexies into rows. Do not press the seams. FIG. L

5. Sew the rows together the same way as with English paper piecing—folding the rows back and forth over themselves and starting and stopping at the X points with lockstitches. Never sew into the seam allowances. FIGS. M-O

6. Press all the horizontal seams down and all the diagonal seams to one side.

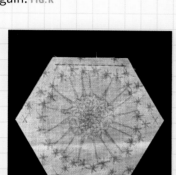

K

Machine stitched from X to X

L

M

Stitched seam

N

O

Helloooo Hexie! Floor Pillow

FINISHED HEXAGON: 3½″ width per side
FINISHED PILLOW: 30″ × 35″ unstuffed

Skill Builders

Fussy cutting hexagons

Strip set construction

Joining hexagons by machine

Floor pillow construction

In a house where quilt forts are a regular occurrence, giant floor pillows can definitely come in handy!

Materials

I've fussy-cut some of the fabrics. Please note that if you plan on fussy cutting you will need extra fabric depending on the size of the fabric repeat. • Fabric requirements are based on 40˝ width of fabric unless otherwise noted. Fat eighths are 9˝ × 21˝.

Focus fabric: 1 fat eighth for the center

Black small print: ⅝ yard

Aqua small print: ⅛ yard

Pink small print: ⅛ yard

Large prints: ½ yard aqua, ½ yard pink for fussy-cut flowers

Muslin: 43˝–44˝ wide, 1⅛ yards

Premade pink piping: 3 yards (or 1 fat eighth and 3 yards of ¼˝ cording)

Backing: 1⅜ yards of home decor weight, canvas, or denim

Batting: 38˝ × 43˝

Other supplies

Pillow stuffing: An old feather duvet is perfect for this. Or use loose polyfill—if you do, make an insert to keep the polyfill in place.

Paper, card stock or template plastic: To make templates

Denim 90/14 sewing machine needle

Cutting

Black small print

• Cut 4 strips 3½˝ × width of fabric for strip sets and half-hexagons

• Cut 2 strips 2˝ × width of fabric for strip sets.

Aqua small print: Cut 2 strips 1½˝ × width of fabric for strip sets.

Pink small print: Cut 2 strips 1˝ × width of fabric for strip sets.

Large prints (aqua and pink)

No need to cut strips if you are fussy-cutting, like I did.

• From *each* print, cut 2 strips 6½˝ × width of fabric.

Muslin: Cut 1 rectangle 38˝ × 43˝

Piping: Cut 6 strips 1¼˝ × 21˝.

Backing: Cut 2 rectangles 23˝ × 38˝.

Construction

Seam allowances are ¼˝ unless otherwise noted.

Preparation

*For more information about making templates, refer to Handy Tips, Techniques, and Terminology, **Making a Template** (page 117).*

1. Make 2 templates from the Mega Hexagon pattern (pullout page P1). The seam allowance is included on this pattern. Cut 1 template in half to make the half-hexagons.

2. Fussy-cut 1 mega hexagon from the focus print for the center.

3. Cut 6 mega hexagons from each of the large prints, 12 total.

4. Cut 12 half-hexagons from 2 of the 3½˝-wide strips of the black small print.

Making the Strip Sets

For more detailed information about strip set construction, refer to **Strip Sets** (page 112).

1. Sew *1 strip set* together from the small print strips in this order:

   a. 3½˝ black   **c.** 1˝ pink

   b. 1½˝ aqua   **d.** 2˝ black

2. Repeat Step 1, *but* use only an 8˝ length from each remaining small print strip. Sew the 8˝ lengths in the same order as Step 1. The remainder of each strip is extra.

3. Using the Mega Hexagon template, cut 6 hexies from the strip sets.

Pillow Assembly

Another easy one to assemble! For more detailed instructions about marking and sewing hexagons together, refer to Machine Piecing (page 72). Lay out the hexies as shown in the pillow top assembly diagram. FIG.A

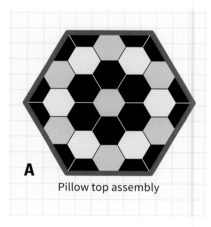

A

Pillow top assembly

TIP

Sewing with half-hexies is easy. They go together exactly the same as whole hexies. You just have to pay a bit more attention when grabbing them to sew. It's easy to get one turned around!

Finishing

1. Layer the pillow top with batting and muslin. Quilt as desired. See **Quilt Finishing** (page 117).

2. Cut off the excess batting and muslin.

3. Press under 1″ on the 38″ edge of a pillow backing rectangle. Press under 1″ again to enclose the raw edge, then topstitch in place. Repeat for the other pillow backing rectangle.

4. To trim the backs to size, lay 1 backing rectangle horizontally right side up, hemmed edge positioned at the bottom with the long raw edge at the top. Place the hexie pillow front right side down on the backing, aligning and centering it with the top edge. Using the pillow front as a template, trim away the excess pillow backing fabric.

5. Repeat Step 4 to trim excess from the second pillow backing, *but this time* have the long raw edge of the backing on the bottom. Align and center the pillow front on the bottom edge and trim.

6. Set both pillow backings aside.

7. Starting in the middle of the bottom edge of the pillow top, align the raw edges of the piping with the edges of the pillow front. Leaving a short tail at the start, pin the piping around all 6 sides. Make gentle curves at each corner and overlap the end with another little tail where you started.

FIG. B

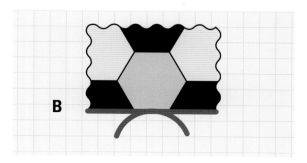

B

8. Baste in place with ⅛″ seam allowance.

9. Layer and pin the pieces in this order:

  a. Pillow top, right side up

  b. First pillow backing rectangle, right side down, hemmed edge lying horizontally as before, and raw edges lined up at the top

  c. Second pillow backing rectangle, right side down, hemmed edge lying horizontally, and raw edges lined up on the bottom (The hemmed edges of the backings should overlap.)

10. Using a zipper foot and with the needle in the leftmost position, sew around all 6 sides with the edge of the zipper foot tight against the piping. Overlock the edges, or run a zigzag stitch on all edges to keep things tidy.

11. Turn right side out and press.

Now stuff it with an old feather duvet or comforter for a squishy finish and jump on!

Snap-Flap Notebook Cover

FINISHED HEXAGON: 1″ width per side

FINISHED NOTEBOOK COVER: 8½″ × 10½″

Skill Builders

English paper piecing

Easy straight-stitch machine appliqué

Working with cork

Making a free-swing pocket

Notebook cover construction

Inserting snaps

I love graph-paper notebooks, for everything. There's something about all those perfectly aligned little boxes that make me want to scribble in them, or fill them with color or even just scratch in some notes. Ninety-nine percent of all my design work starts on simple graph paper. And all my notebooks definitely show the frequent use. So of course I needed to come up with something to protect my plans for world domination, mwahahaha! I mean. Um. Nothing. You heard nothing! Moving along …

Materials

Fabric requirements are based on 40″ width of fabric unless otherwise noted. Fat eighths are 9″ × 21″.

Assorted scraps: 17 scraps minimum 2¾″ × 2¾″ for hexie pocket

Striped fabric: 1 fat eighth for hexie cover wrap

Cork fabric: 1 rectangle 18″ × 27″ for notebook cover (Also called *cork leather*, cork fabric is similar to vinyl and can be sewn as you would vinyl.)

Pocket back: 1 square 10″ × 10″

Pocket lining: 1 fat eighth

Snap-flap: 2 charm squares 5″ × 5″

Other supplies

Fusible woven interfacing: 10″ × 10″ square (such as Pellon SF101)

Medium- to heavyweight interfacing: Scrap, minimum 1½″ square for snap (I generally just use a scrap of denim for this.)

Water-soluble pen: Or other nonpermanent marking tool

Wonder Clips

Hera Marker

Decorative snap: Just 1

EPP papers: 28 count, 1″ hexagon

Cutting

Assorted scraps: Trim scraps to 17 squares 2¾″ × 2¾″.

Cork

• Cut 1 rectangle 11¼″ × 17¾″.

• Cut 2 rectangles 8″ × 11¼″.

Pocket back: Cut 1 rectangle 5¾″ × 7¾″.

Pocket lining: Cut 1 rectangle 5¾″ × 15″.

Snap-flap: Cut 2 rectangles 3″ × 4½″

Fusible woven interfacing

• Cut 1 rectangle 5¾″ × 7¾″ for pocket.

• Cut 2 rectangles 3″ × 4½″ for snap-flap.

Construction

Seam allowances are ¼″ unless otherwise noted. Topstitch ⅛″ from the edge.

Preparation

1. Follow the instructions for Hexagon Block Construction, English Paper Piecing (page 71).

2. Cut 2 of the EPP papers in half across the widest point, from point to point.

3. From the assorted scraps rectangles, cut 13 hexies using the template; and cut 4 half-hexies using the half-EPP paper as the template.

4. From the striped fabric fussy-cut 13 hexies using the template. Set these aside for the cover wrap.

Making the Pocket

1. Arrange 13 hexies and 4 half-hexies in columns in a 3 • 4 • 3 • 4 • 3 pattern, with the columns of 4, counting the half-hexies on top and bottom as one each. FIG. A

2. When you finish the assembly, press the seam allowances open and carefully remove the papers. Press the seam allowance out on all the unsewn exterior edges of the hexies.

3. Center the 5¾″ × 7¾″ interfacing rectangle, fusible side down, on the wrong side of the pocket front. Fuse in place following the manu-facturer's instructions. Trim the overhanging hexies from the sides. FIG. B

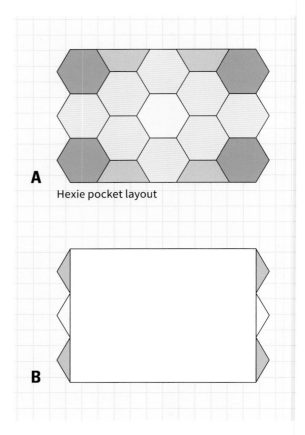

A

Hexie pocket layout

B

TIP

If you want to do any quilting or fancy stitching on the pocket front, it needs to happen right after the interfacing has been fused on.

4. With the hexie pocket front right side up, place the 5¾″ × 7¾″ pocket back rectangle right side down and stitch along the right-hand side. Press open. FIG.C

5. Lay the pocket lining on the pocket front, right sides together. Stitch along the top edge. Turn right side out and press. *Topstitch* (page 116) along the top edge. FIG.D

6. Fold the pocket in half vertically, with the pieced hexies and pocket back rectangle facing. Stitch along the bottom edge and overcast if desired.

7. Turn right side out and press. Baste the left side closed with an ⅛″ seam allowance. Using a Hera marker and starting from one side, make vertical lines every ¾″. Sew along all lines, making sure to lockstitch at the start and end. Set the pocket aside. FIG.E

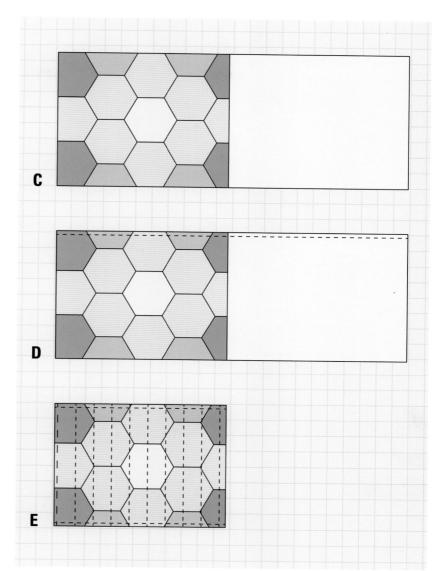

C

D

E

TIP

The ¾″ gap leaves enough room for each slot to hold 2 standard pencils, or one marker. But, depending on what you plan to put in the pencil pocket, you may want to adjust the spacing between seams. Just something to consider before sewing!

Preparing the Cover

Making the Hexie Cover Wrap

1. Arrange the 13 striped hexies as shown and sew together to make a hexie cover wrap. **FIG.F**

> ## TIP
>
> Of course, you don't have to arrange the hexies as shown. I arranged them this way with the stripes aligned because I love to fussy cut directional prints. I mean, I love a good fussy-cut flower or cute animal, but when it comes down to it, it's all about directional prints for me!
>
> You could make the cover entirely out of hexies! Or make 3 vertical stripes with hexies, or even leave the hexies off for that matter, gasp!! Make it you; this is what this is all about right?

2. Once the hexies are sewn together, press and carefully remove the papers. Press again, making sure all the seam allowances stay folded under.

3. Lay the hexie cover wrap right side up on the cover. The bottom points of the hexies should be 2″ from the bottom edge, and the left side should be flush with left side of the cover. There will be about a ¼″ gap on the right edge. Carefully glue-baste in place. Use tiny dots of glue, only in the seam allowance. Do not use pins as the holes will stay in the cork.

4. Appliqué around the entire hexie cover wrap. I like to appliqué by topstitching as close as I can to the edges. **FIG.G**

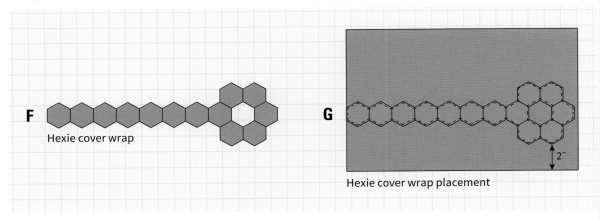

F Hexie cover wrap

G Hexie cover wrap placement

2″

Making the Snap-Flap

Use the Medium Hexagon pattern (pullout page P1).

1. Make a snap-flap *template* (page 117).

2. Following the manufacturer's instructions, apply snap-flap interfacing to the wrong side of both pieces of snap-flap fabric. Using the Snap-Flap template, cut 1 shape from each piece.

3. With right sides together, sew around the snap-flap shape, starting about ½″ from the bottom and ending again a ½″ from the bottom, *lockstitching* (page 116) at both start and end. Leave the bottom open for turning.

4. Turn the snap-flap right side out, gently poking the corners out with a chopstick, and press. *Topstitch* (page 116) around all sewn sides. FIG. H

4. Following the manufacturer's instructions, apply the female side of the snap, centering it on the snap-flap. Be sure the top of the snap is on the top of the snap-flap.

5. Place the snap-flap face down on the cover wrap, directly on top of the second hexie from the left. Baste in place with an ⅛″ seam allowance along the left edge of the cover. FIG. I

6. Place a piece of medium-weight to heavy-weight interfacing on the backside of the cork behind the outermost right hexie of the cover wrap. Apply the male side of the snap, centering it on the hexie with interfacing behind it and anchoring it through all layers. FIG. J

Notebook Cover Assembly

1. Fold under ½″ along the 11¼″ side of each 8″ × 11¼″ cork rectangle, using clips to hold. Topstitch along the folded edges to make the cover sleeves.

2. Place 1 cover sleeve right side up with the topstitched edge to the right. Place the hexie pocket right side up on top of the cover sleeve, 1½″ up from the bottom edge, raw edges aligned on the left. Baste in place with a ⅛″ seam allowance along the left edge. FIG. K

3. Lay the front cover right side up with the snap-flap on the left. Place the blank cover sleeve right sides together on top, aligning raw edges on the left side. Use clips to hold. Sew in place along the

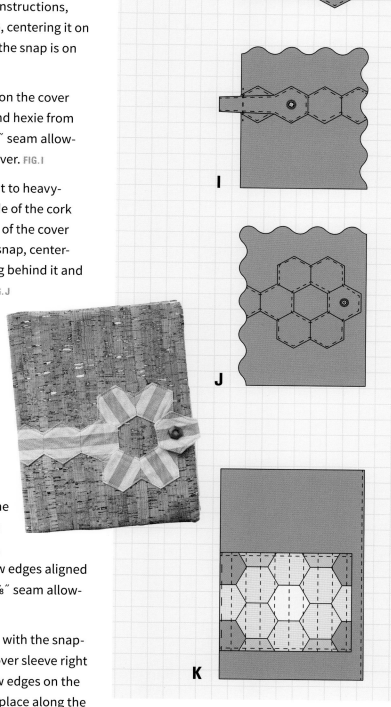

left edge only, lockstitching at the start and finish. Now sew the top and bottom edges separately, starting at the raw edge and stopping at the folded edge each time. Backstitch across the folded edge a few stitches to reinforce.

4. Place the cover sleeve with the pocket right side down on the right-hand side of the front cover and repeat Step 3. **FIG. L**

5. Clip the corners and turn right side out.

6. Fold down the seam allowance in between the cover sleeves and topstitch, making sure to lockstitch at the start and end. **FIG. M**

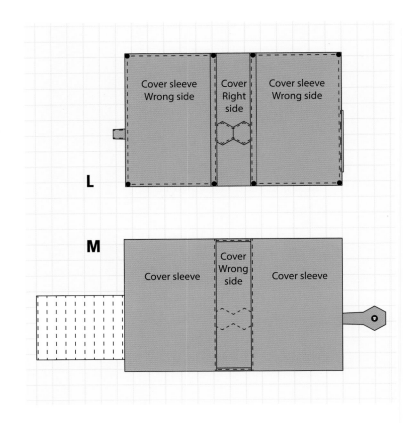

And hey, look at that! When you want to write on the left hand side of the notebook, the fancy pencil pocket conveniently flips out of the way while still being handy! ●

Slide your notebook and some pencils in and get to work!

Flat-Pack Pencil Case

FINISHED HEXAGON: ½″ width per side

FINISHED PENCIL CASE: 6″ × 8″

Skill Builders

English paper piecing (EPP)

Covering raw edges with seam binding

Inserting zippers

Adding a magnetic snap

The perfect pencil case to see everything you have. The double-zip flap allows it to open right up. Pair that with the flat-pack construction, everything stays laid out on display!

Materials

Fabric requirements are based on 40″ width of fabric unless otherwise noted. Fat eighths are 9″ × 21″.

Assorted scraps: 79 scraps minimum 1¾″ × 1¾″ square for hexie panels

Cork fabric or vinyl: 1 square 9″ × 9″ for exterior

Cotton print: 1 fat eighth for lining and seam binding

Other supplies

Fusible woven interfacing: 15″ wide, ⅛ yard (such as Pellon SF101)

Water-soluble pen: Or similar nonpermanent marking tool

Zippers: 2, each 12″ long

Heavy interfacing: Scrap minimum 1½″ × 3″ for magnet (If you don't have heavy interfacing on hand, denim would work.)

Sew-in magnetic snap

Wonder Clips

EPP papers: 79 count, ½″ hexagon

Cutting

Cotton print

• Cut 1 rectangle 3½″ × 8¾″ and 1 rectangle 3¼″ × 4½″.

• Cut 2 strips 1½″ × 7″ for seam binding.

Fusible woven interfacing: Cut 1 rectangle 3½″ × 8¾″ and 1 rectangle 3¼″ × 4½″.

Heavy interfacing: Cut 2 squares 1½″ × 1½″.

Construction

Seam allowances are ¼″ unless otherwise noted. Topstitch at ⅛″.

Making the Hexie Panels

*If you choose to make your own templates, refer to **Making a Template** (page 117). Use the Micro Hexagon pattern (pullout page P1).*

Follow the instructions in Hexagon Block Construction, English Paper Piecing (page 71), to make 79 hexies from assorted scraps. Make 2 separate panels, a large zipper panel and a small zip-flap panel.

Large Zipper Panel

1. Join 48 hexies in a 10 • 9 • 10 • 9 • 10 hexie-per-column formation.

2. Press the panel well and carefully remove papers.

3. Press open the seam allowances of hexies at both ends of the shorter columns (2 and 4) so they are flush with the hexies in the longer columns (1, 3, and 5).

4. Center the interfacing rectangle 3½″ × 8¾″ on the wrong side of the large zipper panel and fuse in place following the manufacturer's directions. Trim the panel even with the fusible interfacing. FIG. A

If any quilting or fancy stitching is desired on the panel it should be done now.

5. On the right side of the hexie panel, make a mark 2″ down from the top edge and centered from side-to-side. Position a 1½″ square of heavy interfacing behind the mark on the wrong side. Hand sew one side of the magnet snap to the front over the mark. Set panel aside. FIG. B

Small Zip-Flap Panel

1. Join 31 hexies in a 4 • 5 • 4 • 5 • 4 • 5 • 4 hexies-per-column formation.

2. Follow Steps 2–4 of the large zipper panel construction, except use the 3¼″ × 4½″ interfacing rectangle this time.

3. With right sides together, sew the lining rectangle 3¼″ × 4½″ to the hexie panel on 3 sides, leaving a 4½″ side open; this will be the top. **Clip the corners** (page 115), turn right side out, and **topstitch** (page 116) around the 3 sewn sides. FIG. C

4. Slide a 1½″ square of heavy interfacing between the hexie panel and the lining, pushing it against the topstitching and centering it. With the *top of the snap* centered and a ¼″ from the bottom edge, hand sew the other side of the magnetic snap onto the lining side of the zip-flap panel.

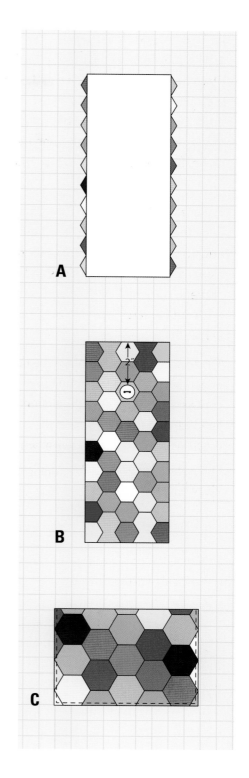

A

B

C

Attaching the Zippers

1. With the large hexie panel right side up, place both zippers face down and with the metal zipper stops 1″ away from the top edge. Pin in place and fold back the tops of the zippers at a 45° angle, pinning them down. Baste both zippers in place using a ⅛″ seam allowance. FIG. D

2. Place the lining fabric right sides together on the zipper panel and sew both sides and across the top edge. Trim off excess zipper at the top on both sides and clip the corners. Turn right side out and carefully push out corners. Topstitch both sides and across the top. FIGS. E-F

3. Close the zippers and place the hexie panel right sides together on top of the cork exterior. Make sure the zipper edge is lined up with the right side of the cork and the hexie panel is aligned with the bottom edge. Clip the zipper in place and open it up so it's easier to sew. FIG. G

> ### TIP
> Wonder clips are super-handy in situations like this. When sewing with cork or vinyl, pins will leave tiny holes that won't go away. With a Wonder clip, you just clip it on and clip it off. No holes!

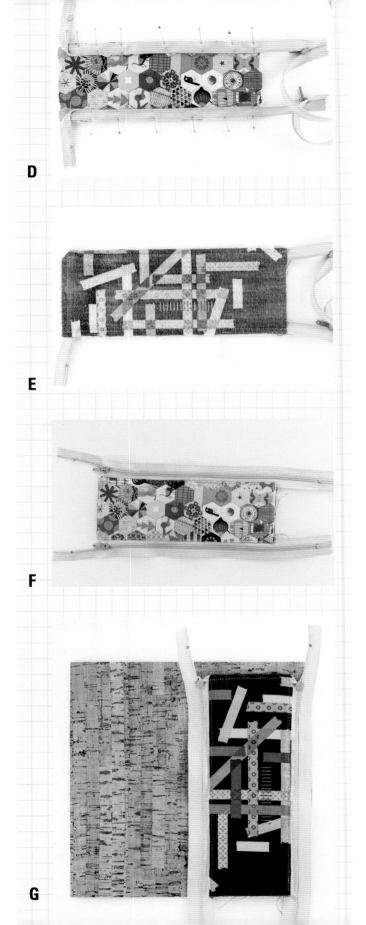

D

E

F

G

4. Sew the zipper in place with a ¼˝ seam allowance. Repeat on the other side. Turn the zipper right side up, folding the cork edge under. Topstitch along the fold. FIGS. H-I

Pencil Case Assembly

1. Mark the center of the cork at the top and the bottom in the seam allowance, and at the bottom of the hexie panel. Line up the 2 center marks at the bottom and clip in place. Stitch with a ¼˝ seam allowance, lockstitching at start and end. Trim off the excess zipper lengths. FIGS. J-K

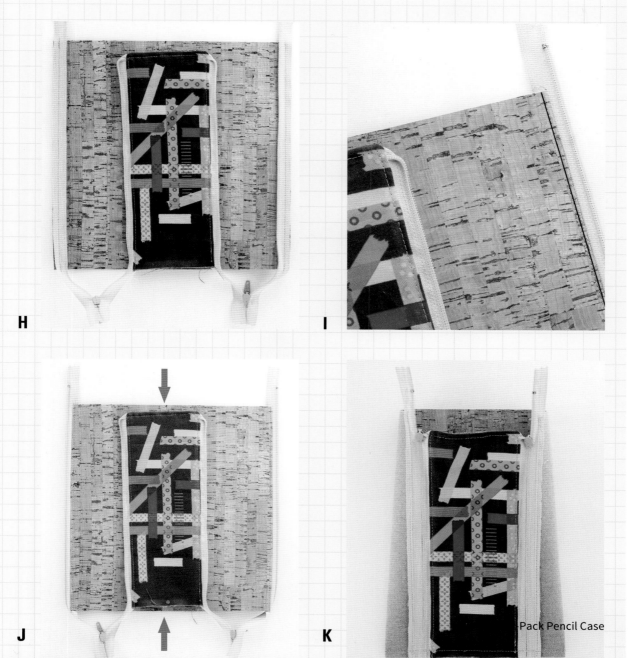

H

I

J

K

2. Mark the center of the small zip-flap panel's raw edge. Right sides together, match the zip-flap's center mark with the center mark on the top edge of the cork panel. Clip in place. Fold the zipper edges over so the zippers sit on top of the zip-flap panel. The topstitched edge of the zipper will touch the edge of the zip-flap panel. Sew across the entire top with a ¼″ seam allowance and trim off the excess zipper lengths. FIGS. L-M

3. Make seam binding with the 2 cotton print strips 1½″ × 7″. See *Seam Binding* (page 114).

4. Wrap the raw edges on both ends of the pencil case with the seam binding, making sure the seam binding ends are folded under and stitch in place. Hand stitch the ends of the seam binding closed. FIG. N

5. Finish by topstitching across seam binding on both ends in between the zippers to hold the binding down. FIG. O

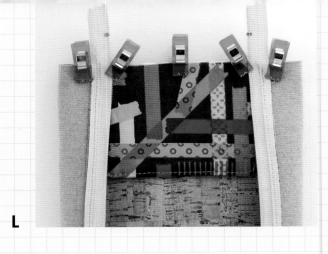

L

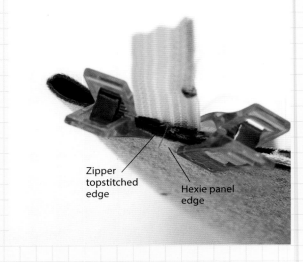

Zipper topstitched edge

Hexie panel edge

M

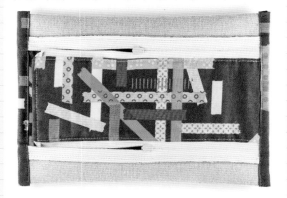

N

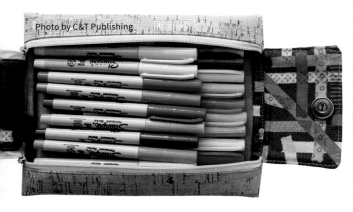

Fill it up with your favorite markers and see how easy every color is to find!

O

6

New York Beauty

In a New York minute!

In a New York Minute is how quickly I fell in love with New York Beauty blocks. Not how fast it is to make them; They're definitely not for the faint of heart! Foundation paper piecing, mixed with all kinds of bias and, hey, let's throw in some curved piecing while we're at it! Yikes! Sound fun? How about you give it a try and see! It will be worth it in the end, trust me!

NEW YORK BEAUTY

BLOCK 92

Mega Project

Half-Moon Mat   98

Medium Project

Pop-Apart Project Pouch   101

Micro Project

Phat Flat Pinnie   107

NEW YORK BEAUTY BLOCK

Some people prefer to just grab pieces of fabric and sew them in place with foundation paper piecing; others prefer to have all their pieces precut to size so they know they're going to fit. I fall somewhere in between. For repeating patterns, such as the New York Beauty block, I like to have my pieces cut to size and ready to go, so I've included specific measurements for each size of block. Don't feel that you have to use these measurements; it's just how I like to do it! If you are using the measurements, note that

they offer a bit of wiggle room so it's not necessary to line everything up perfectly! And some of them will seem dramatically larger than necessary. Angles, people! When foundation paper-piecing with angles, more fabric makes things so much easier!

Block Essentials

This is what is needed to make the sample block. All individual sizes are included with the actual projects.

Section A: 4 squares of background (white-and-black print)

Section B:

• 20 rectangles of background (white-and-black print)

• 24 rectangles of color (chartreuse)

Section C:

• 20 rectangles of background (white-and-black print)

• 24 rectangles of color (assorted blues and 1 peach)

Section D:

• 20 rectangles of background (white-and-black print)

• 24 rectangles of color (assorted blues and 1 peach)

Section E: 4 corners of background (white-and-black print)

Foundation papers: I print all my foundation paper piecing patterns on standard printer/copy paper, but many companies make specialty paper for foundation paper-piecing (including Simple Foundations Translucent

Vellum Paper and Carol Doak's Foundation Paper, both from C&T Publishing). This choice comes down to personal preference, so my suggestion is try what you have available to you and go from there!

Thread: I recommend InvisaFil (by Wonderfil Specialty Threads) for foundation paper piecing. For the construction of the project and quilting, I recommend Aurifil 50-weight thread.

Seam roller (optional)

Glue stick

New York Beauty Block Construction

Make 4 foundation paper copies of New York Beauty pattern sections B, C, and D; and 2 templates from New York Beauty pattern sections A and E.

A few things before we begin.

- I like to make notes directly on my patterns or even quickly color in sections so I know what fabric is going where. This is especially important if you want the same print or color to match up when sections are sewn together.

- I also mark each section being sewn together with the same number on the pattern so when I go to sew all the sections together, I know that they are all supposed to go together.

- Lower your stitch length to about 1.5–1.8 mm. This will perforate the paper, making it easier to pull off at the end.

- Seam allowances are included in the patterns.

- Sections A and E are not pieced. Make **templates** (page 117) from these pattern pieces and use to cut the background fabric.

Sewing the Sections

Please note that I've started with section C of the pattern. As long as you work each lettered section numerically, the instructions are the same and you can start with whichever section you like!

1. Place the C1 background rectangle, right side up, on top of piece C1 on the unprinted side of the pattern. Make sure that the fabric covers the whole section plus a minimum of ¼″ all the way around. Hold the pattern piece with the fabric up to a light source to see if there is full coverage. Use a smidge of glue stick to hold it in place. **FIG.A**

A

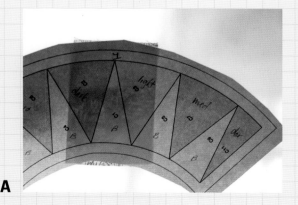

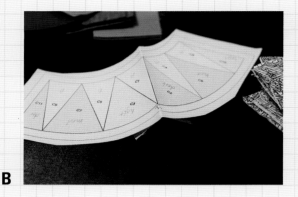

B

C

2. Fold the paper on the line between C1 and C2. The fold indicates the sewing line. Place the C2 color rectangle right sides together, on top of the C1 piece, making sure that the edge is ¼˝ over the fold. Make sure that when folded back along the seamline, the C2 fabric will cover section C2 plus a minimum ¼˝ all the way around. FIGS. B-D

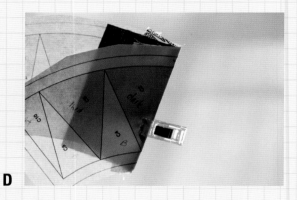

D

3. On the printed side of the paper, sew on the marked line in between C1 and C2, making sure to extend by about ¼˝ past the end of the seamline. FIG. E

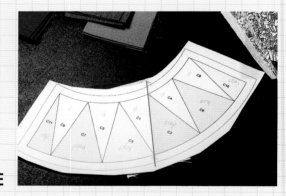

E

F

G

4. Fold back the paper and trim the seam allowance to ¼˝. Flip the C2 fabric rectangle in place and press. I use a seam roller for pressing. It cuts down drastically on the amount of time traveling to the iron! FIGS.F-G

5. Continue, repeating Steps 2–4 until the entire section is complete. FIG.H

6. Press well and trim back to the seam allowance, using a ruler for the sides and freehand on the curves. FIG.I

H

> ### TIP
> Using a smaller rotary cutter for the curves will make things infinitely easier. I have a 28 mm rotary cutter just for cutting curves.

7. Carefully remove the paper from the back and press again. FIG.J

8. Repeat Steps 1–7 for sections B, C, and D.

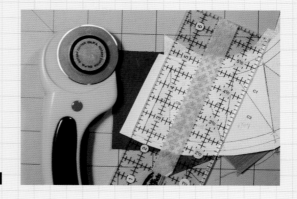

I

J

Assembling the Sections

Assemble sections together in the order you prefer. I started with sections C and D, then added section B to section C, pieced A to section B, and finally pieced E to section D. The order in which they're sewn together doesn't matter as long as when they're connected, they all line up in alphabetical order.

1. With right sides together, match the center points of sections C and D by sliding a pin into the point on the wrong side of section D and into the matching point on section C. Push the pin flush and add a second pin to hold in place. Working out from the center, continue matching points and adding pins. Repeat on the other side of the center point. Fill in with more pins to keep the seams together. Then add more pins … and maybe one more. **FIGS. K-L**

2. Reset the stitch setting on your sewing machine to the regular stitch length and sew with a ¼˝ seam allowance. One of the sections will ruffle when everything is pinned in place; sew with the ruffled section up.

> ### TIP
> Depending on the curve, you may want to shorten your stitch length a little. The tighter the curve the shorter your stitch length should be.

3. Press toward section D. **FIG. M**

4. Repeat Steps 1 and 2 to add section B to section C. Press to section B.

K

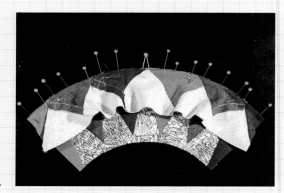

L

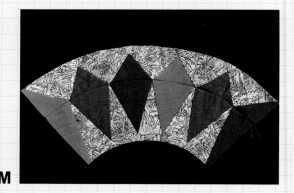

M

5. Find the center of piece A by folding it in half and finger-pressing. With right sides together, line up the center of piece A with the center of section B and pin. Line up the sides and pin, then pin along the curve, easing the 2 pieces together. FIG. N

N

6. Sew A & B together using a ¼˝ seam allowance with the ruffled section on the top. Press to piece A.

7. Repeat Steps 5 and 6 to sew piece E to section D. Press to piece E.

TIP

You may need to add in a few more marks on piece E to help align it with piece D. To do this, fold piece E in half and finger-press a line. Open and fold both sides into the center, then finger-press 2 more lines.

Repeat the process for section D and use the lines to match up.

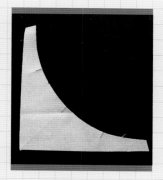

8. You now have 1 quarter-block. To make a complete circle, add 3 more quarter-blocks and sew together in pairs. Press the seams open and sew pairs together. Press the seams open.

Half-Moon Mat

FINISHED QUARTER-BLOCK: 15″ × 15″
FINISHED MAT: 15″ × 30″

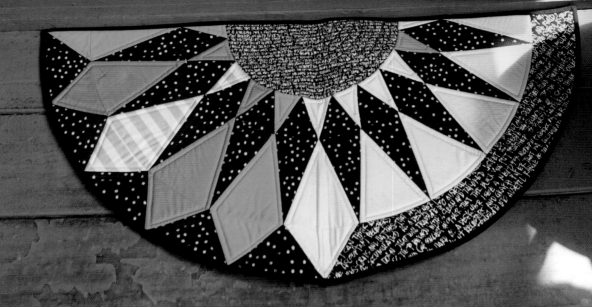

Skill Builders

Foundation paper piecing

Curved piecing

Quilt finishing

Using an alternative to batting

Bias binding

We're going to mix things up a bit with this one. Why follow the rules right? So for this one, we are going to cover several individual sections of the pattern with one large piece of fabric. Just because the pattern lines are there doesn't mean you need to use them all!

Materials

Fabric requirements are based on 40˝ width of fabric unless otherwise noted.

Assorted black prints: 1 yard total for background

Assorted blues: ¾ yard total

Binding: 1 fat quarter (or you could use other yardage)

Backing: ⅔ yard

Batting: 19˝ × 34˝

Other supplies

Thread: I recommend InvisaFil (by Wonderfil Specialty Threads).

Seam roller (optional)

Glue stick

Foundation papers

Cutting

Assorted black prints

• Cut 1 rectangle 5½˝ × 10½˝ for section A.

• Cut 10 squares 3½˝ × 3½˝ for section B.

• Cut 10 rectangles 4½˝ × 6˝ for section C.

• Cut 5 squares 4½˝ × 4½˝ and 1 rectangle 7˝ × 22½˝ for section D.

Assorted blues

• Cut 12 squares 3½˝ × 3½˝ total for section B.

• Cut 12 rectangles 4½˝ × 6˝ total for section C.

• Cut 7 squares 4½˝ × 4½˝ total for section D.

Backing: Cut 1 rectangle 19˝ × 34˝.

Construction

Seam allowances are ¼˝ unless otherwise noted. Make 2 foundation paper copies of Mega New York Beauty pattern sections B, C, and D (pullout page P2); and 1 template from Mega New York Beauty pattern section A (pullout page P1). Omit section E.

Assembly

1. Follow the instructions in New York Beauty Block Construction (page 93), but with the following changes:

- Fold the 5½″ × 10½″ rectangle in half and place the fold line indicated from template A on the fold. Cut and open.

- For 1 quarter-block, assemble only sections B, C and D.

- For the second quarter-block, piece sections B and C as per instructions. For section D, position the 7″ × 22½″ background rectangle to cover the entire arc. At the end of the arc, stitch a blue section D square for D10. Trim this section as if it was fully pieced.

2. Join sections B, C, and D for both quarter-blocks.

3. Sew the quarter-blocks together and press the seam open.

4. Sew piece A to sections B, marking the center point and quarter points as done in piece E in New York Beauty Block Construction, Assembling the Sections, Steps 5–8 (page 97). Press the seam allowances toward A.

Finishing

1. Before proceeding, prepare at least 90″ of 2″ *double-fold bias binding* (page 113).

2. Layer, quilt, and bind as desired. See *Quilt Finishing* (page 117).

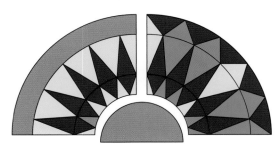

Mat assembly

> ### TIP
> Instead of batting, try using a towel. It's more absorbent and will thicken up the mat a bit. Or try a thin foam, such as Pellon FF77 Flex-Foam or ByAnnie's Soft and Stable.

Pop-Apart Project Pouch

FINISHED BLOCK: 12″ × 12″

FINISHED POUCH: 15″ × 45″ (opened fully) / 15″ × 15″ (closed)

Skill Builders

Foundation paper piecing

Curved piecing

Quilting

Adding decorative snaps

Tool pocket construction

The perfect pouch to take along to a class or sewing day! This pouch holds a 12½″ ruler and rotating cutting mat, plus has plenty of pockets for all the tools you need. And when you pop open the flap, there's a handy pressing mat! So go on, sign up for that sewing retreat, you deserve it!

Materials

Fabric requirements are based on 40″ width of fabric unless otherwise noted.

Aqua: 1½ yards for pouch lining, cutting mat pocket, and lining

White with black print: 1 yard for block background and pouch exterior

Black print: ½ yard, or use 2 fat quarters if you want different fabrics for tools pocket

Note | I didn't have enough black fabric for the tool pocket, so I added a thin chartreuse strip to make a pieced pocket instead. The directions are for a plain pocket as I originally intended, but feel free to make your own pieced fabric for the pockets!

Assorted blues: ½ yard

Chartreuse: 1 fat eighth

Pink (accent): 1 scrap minimum 6″ × 6″ square

Binding: ¼ yard black with white print

Other supplies

Fusible woven interfacing: 15″ wide, 1¼ yards (such as 1 package of Pellon SF101)

Silver heat-resistant fabric: 44″ wide, ½ yard (such as Therma-Flec Heat-Resistant Fabric, by James Thompson & Co. Inc.) (I used an ironing board cover!)

Foam stabilizer: 1 package, 18″ × 58″ (such as ByAnnie's Soft and Stable)

Thread: I recommend InvisaFil (by Wonderfil Specialty Threads).

Seam roller (optional)

Glue stick

Foundation papers

Decorative snaps: 4

Cutting

Aqua

• Cut 3 strips 15″ × width of fabric.

From 1 strip, subcut 1 rectangle 15″ × 30¼″ for pouch lining.

From 2 strips, subcut 2 rectangles 15″ × 27″ for cutting mat pocket exterior and lining.

White with black print

• Cut 1 strip 15″ × width of fabric; subcut 1 rectangle 15″ × 31¾″ for pouch exterior.

• Cut 4 strips 2″ × width of fabric.

From 1 strip, subcut 20 rectangles 2″ × 1½″ for section B.

From 3 strips, subcut 20 rectangles 2″ × 3″ for section C and 20 rectangles 2″ × 2½″ for section D.

• Cut 1 strip 1¾″ × width of fabric; subcut into 1 strip 1¾″ × 15″ for block bottom border and 2 strips 1¾″ × 12½″ for block side borders.

Black print: Cut 1 strip 15″ × width of fabric; subcut 2 rectangles 15″ × 17½″ for tools pocket exterior and lining.

Assorted blues

• Cut 23 rectangles 2″ × 3″ for section C.

• Cut 23 rectangles 2″ × 2½″ for section D.

Chartreuse: Cut 2 strips 2″ × 21″; subcut 24 rectangles 1½″ × 2″ for section B.

Pink

• Cut 1 rectangle 2″ × 3″ for section C.

• Cut 1 rectangle 2″ × 2½″ for section D.

Binding: Cut 4 strips 2″ × width of fabric.

Fusible woven interfacing

• Cut 1 rectangle 15″ × 27″ for cutting mat pocket.

• Cut 1 rectangle 15″ × 17½″ for tools pocket.

Silver heat-resistant fabric: Cut 1 rectangle 15″ × 15¼″.

Foam stabilizer: Cut 1 rectangle 15″ × 45″.

Construction

Seam allowances are ¼″ unless otherwise noted. Make 4 foundation paper copies of Medium New York Beauty pattern sections B, C, and D (pullout page P2); and 2 templates from Medium New York Beauty pattern sections A and E (pullout page P2).

Block Assembly

1. Using the templates, cut 4 each of sections A and E from the white and black print.

2. Follow the instructions in New York Beauty Block Construction (page 93) to make 1 block. Feel free to make your own color placement choices for the wedges.

Exterior Assembly

Note: If you want the accent wedge to be positioned a certain way on the finished pouch, orient the block accordingly in front of you before starting this section.

1. Sew 2 exterior strips 1¾″ × 12½″ to the opposite sides of the New York Beauty block, pressing away from the block.

2. Sew 1 exterior strip 1¾″ × 15″ to the bottom, pressing away from the block. FIG. A

3. Sew the 15″ × 31¾″ exterior rectangle to the top, unbordered side.

4. Spray baste the foam stabilizer to the wrong side of the exterior and quilt as desired.

Interior Assembly

Pocket Panel

1. Fuse the 2 interfacing rectangles to the wrong side of the pocket linings: cutting mat

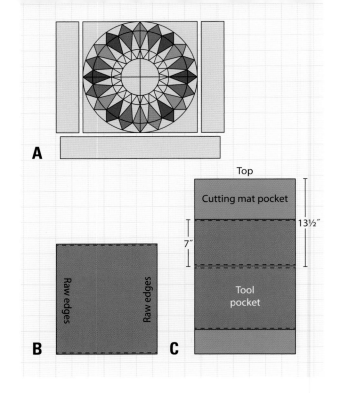

pocket lining (15″ × 27″), and tools pocket lining (15″ × 17½″).

2. Place the tool pocket exterior and lining right sides together and sew across both 15″ sides only. Turn right side out. Press and *topstitch* (page 116) both finished ends. FIG. B

3. Fold the 27″ length of the aqua cutting mat pocket's unlined exterior in half and finger-press at each end of the fold to mark.

4. On the right side of the tools pocket, draw a centerline from side to side with a removable marker, that is parallel to the topstitching, and 7″ down from a finished edge. Whichever edge you choose to measure from becomes the top of the tools pocket.

5. Place the tools pocket on top of the cutting mat pocket fabric, lining up the marked centerline of the tools pocket with the finger-pressed marks on the cutting mat pocket. Topstitch ¼″ on both sides of the marked centerline, joining the 2 pockets. FIG. C

6. Orient the pocket panel from Step 5 vertically in front of you. Remember the top of the tools pocket? Measuring from the left top corner of the tools pocket, mark vertical lines at 3½″, 5½″, 7½″, and 11½″ from the left edge. Stitch the lines, starting at the top of the tools pocket and ending at the top horizontal stitching line. *Lockstitch* (page 116) at the start and finish of each line.

7. Mark a vertical line in the middle of the bottom half of the tools pocket, 7½″ from the left edge. Stitch the line, starting at the bottom horizontal line and ending at the bottom edge of the tools pocket. Lockstitch at the start and finish. FIG.D

8. Pair the pocket panel right sides together with the interfaced cutting mat lining and sew across both 15″ sides. Turn right side out, press, and topstitch. Set aside. FIG.E

Interior Panel

1. Sew the heat-resistant rectangle to a 15″ end of the pouch lining 15″ × 30¼″ right sides together. Press toward the pouch lining and topstitch on the lining side ⅛″ from that seam. The side with the heat-resistant fabric is the top of the interior panel. Just as with the pocket panel (Step 6), orient the pouch lining vertically in front of you. FIG.F

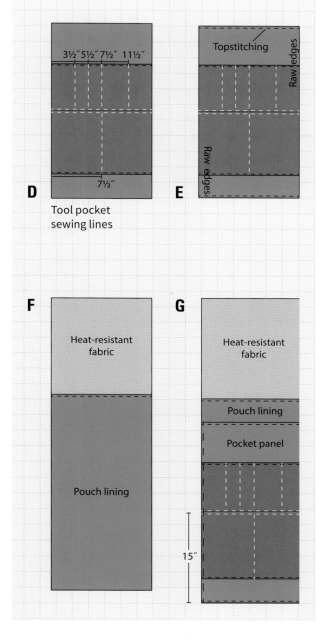

D Tool pocket sewing lines

2. Draw a centerline from side to side on the right side of the pouch lining, 15″ up from the bottom. Lay the pocket panel face up on top of the pouch lining, matching the pocket panel centerline to the centerline of the pouch lining. Clip or pin in place. Baste along each long side ⅛″ from the edge. The interior panel is assembled. FIG.G

Pouch Assembly

1. Lay the exterior panel right side down with the New York Beauty block on the left. Place the interior panel right side up on top with the heat-resistant fabric on the left over the New York Beauty block. Clip and topstitch in place on the centerline of the tools pocket, and across the existing topstitching near the heat-resistant surface (see Interior Panel, Step 1, page 105).

2. Baste the perimeter ⅛″ from the edge.

3. Sew a second stitching line 1″ from the edge using your regular stitch length, but this time, *do not* stitch on the heat-resistant fabric. Stitch only around the edge of the pouch lining/pocket panel. Start and end at the connecting seam between the heat-resistant fabric and the pouch lining, lockstitching at the start and finish.

4. Bind the perimeter. See *Double-Fold Binding* (page 114).

Now load it up with everything you need and go sew! But remember, if you're planning on carrying acrylic rulers, put them in the same pocket as the cutting mat to help keep them safe. There's nothing worse than showing up for a class or retreat and finding your ruler cracked!

Installing the Snaps

1. Following the manufacturer's instructions, attach the 4 female sides of the snaps to the 4 corners of the pouch, sitting just at the edges of the binding. Make sure the decorative side of the snap is on the exterior.

2. Fold the bottom edge up on the stitched centerline of the pocket panels. Mark where the male side of the snap needs to go on both sides and install.

3. Snap the bottom edge shut. Fold the top edge over at the seam between the heat-resistant fabric and interior panel; mark the positions, where the male snaps need to go, and install.

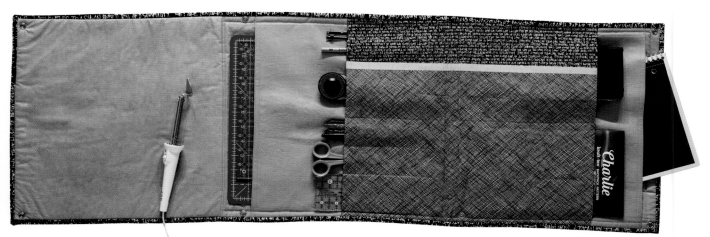

Skill Builders

Foundation piecing in a small format

Stuffing and finishing with flat edge

This pretty pinnie works double duty, holding your pins and giving you a flat edge to slip on some clips so they're always handy!

Materials

Fat eighths are 9″ × 21″.

Black-and-white crosshatch: 1 fat eighth

Chartreuse: 1 square 10″ × 10″

Turquoise: 1 square 10″ × 10″

Pink: 1 square 10″ × 10″

Backing: 1 square 10″ × 10″

Other supplies

Fusible woven interfacing: 1 scrap minimum 6½″ × 6½″ (such as Pellon SF101)

Foundation papers

Thread: I recommend InvisaFil (by Wonderfil Specialty Threads).

Seam roller (optional)

Glue stick

Pincushion filling

Cutting

Black-and-white crosshatch

• Cut 3 strips 1½″ × 21″.

From 2 strips, subcut 12 rectangles 1½″ × 1¾″ for section C and 12 rectangles 1½″ × 1¾″ for section D.

From 1 strip, subcut 12 squares 1½″ × 1½″ for section B.

Chartreuse

• Cut 4 strips 1½″ × 10″.

From 2 strips cut 10 squares 1½″ × 1½″ for section B.

From 2 strips, cut 10 rectangles 1½″ × 1¾″ for section C.

Turquoise: Cut 2 strips 1½″ × 10″; subcut 10 rectangles 1½″ × 1¾″ for section D.

Pink: Cut 2 squares 3½″ × 3½″ for section A.

Construction

Seam allowances are ¼″ unless otherwise noted. Make 2 foundation paper copies of Micro New York Beauty pattern sections B, C, and D (pullout page P2), and 1 template of Micro New York Beauty pattern section A (pullout page P2). Section E is omitted.

Block Assembly

Follow the instructions in New York Beauty Block Construction (page 93) to make 2 quarter-blocks.

1. Using a finished quarter-block as a template, trim the curved edges of the 2 pink 3½″ squares.

2. Sew the 4 quarters together into pairs, pressing toward the pink.

3. Sew the pairs together and press the seam open.

Finishing

1. Cut the interfacing to a circle using the finished block as a template. Following the manufacturer's instructions, fuse interfacing to the wrong side of the block.

Now stick it full of pins, clip it up, and get sewing!

> **TIP**
>
> Interfacing could just as easily be swapped out for batting or fusible fleece if you wanted. It will, however, make the clip strip around the perimeter puffy. Not bad, just puffy.

2. Place the fused circle right sides together on the 6½″ backing square. Sew around the perimeter, leaving a 2″ gap for turning. Cut away the backing fabric around the circle edges. FIG. A

3. Notch the perimeter with pinking shears or by snipping V's into the seam allowance. Be careful not to snip the seam.

4. Turn right side out and gently push out the seam with a chopstick.

5. *Topstitch* (page 116) ½″ from the edge around three quarters of the pinnie, lockstitching at the start and finish.

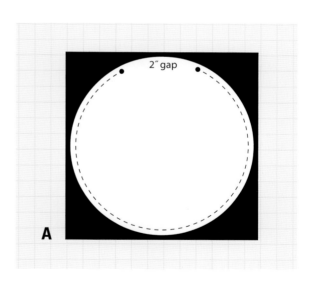

2″ gap

A

6. Fill with crushed walnut shells or choice of pincushion filling and hand stitch the opening closed.

7. Finish topstitching the last quarter of the pinnie ½″ from the edge to complete the clip flange.

GLOSSAPENDIUM!

Handy Tips, Techniques, and Terminology

Basic Blocks

Half-Square Triangles

HALF-SQUARE TRIANGLES: 2-IN-1 METHOD

This method is great for when you want all your half-square triangles to be made with different fabrics.

Place 2 squares right sides together and draw a diagonal line from corner to corner on the back of 1 square. Sew a scant ¼˝ seam on each side of the line. Cut on the line and press both open. Square up to the size needed.

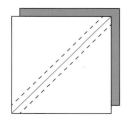

2-in-1 half-square triangles

HALF-SQUARE TRIANGLES: 4-IN 1 METHOD

Place 2 squares right sides together and sew around all 4 sides with a ¼˝ seam allowance. Cut a diagonal line from corner to corner. Without moving the fabric, cut a second diagonal line from the opposite corners. Press the seams open and square up to the desired size.

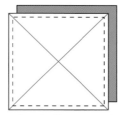

4-in-1 half-square triangles

HALF-SQUARE TRIANGLES: 8-IN-1 METHOD

Place 2 squares right sides together and draw an X from corner to corner on the back of 1 square. Sew a ¼˝ seam on each side of both drawn lines. Cut on the drawn X, and without moving the fabric, cut horizontally and vertically through the center of the square. Press the seams open and square up to the desired size.

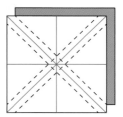

8-in-1 half-square triangles

Corner-Square Triangles

These are most commonly seen in snowball blocks but can be fun in so many more.

Lay a square of fabric over the corner to be removed. Sew a diagonal line from corner to corner. Trim the seam allowance to ¼˝ and press open.

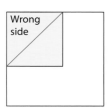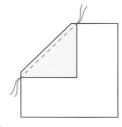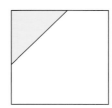

Corner-square triangle

Strip Sets

A strip set is a group of fabric strips that have been sewn together and then subcut into small segments.

Sew the strips of fabric together lengthwise. If you're sewing multiple strips together, start each seam at the opposite end of the seam before to keep the strip set from bowing. Press the seams as desired. I like to press the seams open when sewing more than 2 or 3 strips together; otherwise I press them to one side. Subcut the strip set into the required segments.

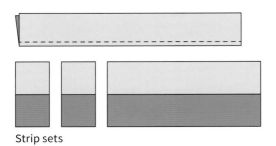

Strip sets

Four-Patch Units

These are dead-easy to make and so versatile in the projects.

Sew 4 squares of fabric right sides together into 2 pairs. Press the seams as indicated by the arrows. Sew the 2 pairs together. If the seams are pressed in alternate directions, they will nest tightly together! Press the final seam open.

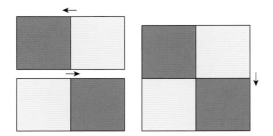

Four-patch

Nine-Patch Units

This is another great basic. They go together fast and work beautifully as a filler block in quilts. Or even on their own!

Sew 3 rows of 3 squares together and press the seams as indicated by the arrows. Sew the rows together.

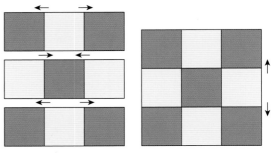

Nine-patch

Basting

Machine baste   A long stitch length (5.0 mm) used to temporarily hold fabrics together. This is helpful when you have more than 2 layers to sew in place. Basting one section to another will keep it from getting unruly while you wrestle another section into place! Make sure you always baste within the seam allowance.

Glue baste   To glue something in place temporarily until it can be stitched. I glue baste everything! Everything that I appliqué is glue basted first. I glue baste seams to keep tricky points matched while sewing blocks together, bindings for hand sewing, bindings for machine sewing, the touch panel of my sewing machine once, English paper pieces—I think you get the idea here. For what I like to use, see *Fabric Glue* (page 120).

Spray baste   To hold the layers of a quilt together (see *Spray Adhesive*, page 122). For more information on quilt basting, see *Quilt Finishing* (page 117).

Binding

Binding is used to cover the outer raw edges of a quilt or project.

Straight-Grain Binding

These fabric binding strips are cut along the grain of the fabric, crosswise (selvage to selvage) or lengthwise (raw edge to raw edge) This type of binding is perfect for square-cornered quilts and projects when the corners will be mitered.

Double-Fold Bias Binding

Bias binding is cut along the bias of the fabric, on a 45° angle from the straight grain. This is the type of binding you want to use around curves, as the fabric stretches easily on the bias.

Once you have bias strips cut, see Double-Fold Binding (page 114) to make them for your project.

How Much Binding Do You Need?

First, find the perimeter of your project. Measure all 4 sides of your project, add them up, and add extra for connecting. I usually add an extra 10″. This is the length you need.

To find out how many strips of straight-grain binding to cut, divide the length of binding by the width of the fabric you are going to use. For a 60″ × 70″ quilt, the math would be:

60″ + 60″ + 70″ + 70″ + 10″ = 270″ of binding

To see how many binding strips to cut:

270″ ÷ 40″ (usable width of fabric) = 6.75 strips; rounded up would be 7 strips

Calculating yardage for bias-cut binding is a little trickier and requires slightly more intense math. It's truly just easier to use the size square I give you in the pattern and reference the C&T website for how to proceed (go to ctpub.com > *scroll down to* Support: Quiltmaking Basics and Sewing Tips > Calculating Yardage for Bias Binding).

Diagonal Seams

I prefer my binding strips sewn together on a 45° angle. There's less bulk at the seams this way.

1. Lay the strips right sides together with the ends perpendicular to each other.

2. Draw a line from the upper left corner of the top strip down to reach the bottom right corner of the bottom strip.

3. Sew on the line and trim the seam allowance to ¼″.

4. Press the seam open and continue on to the next strip.

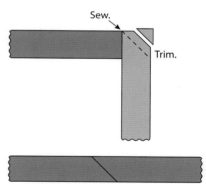

Attaching binding strips at a 45° angle

Double-Fold Binding

This is the most common and easiest type of binding to make, usually made from 2″ to 2½″ strips of fabric, straight grain or bias. I use 2″ strips for all my bindings, just personal preference; I like skinny bindings. But if you're new to the binding game, 2½″ is more commonly used and easier to get the hang of. Fold the entire length of binding strips in half and press. You now have double-fold binding! But wait, there's only one fold? The second fold happens after the binding is sewn to your project and is folded over the seam allowance.

See **Quilt Finishing** (page 117) for information on attaching your binding to your project.

Seam Binding (Single-Fold Binding)

Seam binding and double-fold binding are essentially doing the same thing (covering raw edges), but differ in how they are doing it and how they are made. With a standard double-fold quilt binding, you align the raw edges of the folded binding with the raw edges of the quilt, stitch by machine, then wrap the folded edge of the binding around the raw edges of the quilt and sew it down again. This creates 2 layers of fabric on the quilt edge for durability. Seam binding, which I've used to enclose the raw edges of the Double-Strap Market Sack (page 12) and the inner seams of the Flat-Pack Pencil Case (page 85), is a single-fold binding that has its edges folded to finish. To use it, you insert the seam between the folded edges of the seam binding, encasing the seam allowance, then machine stitch the front and back of the binding all at once. I find seam binding handy on smaller projects where you need to enclose a seam and don't want the hassle of sewing a double-fold binding, which requires sewing it twice.

Seam binding can also be referred to as bias tape when made with bias-cut strips.

I'll be honest and say I rarely use bias tape—seam binding yes, but bias tape, nope. I truly find it easier to make a bias-cut **double-fold binding** (at left) and use that instead.

But try different things and find the way that works for you. There's no right or wrong.

There are many different ways to make seam binding / bias tape, including gadgets that can help you out. I'm going to show you how I made the seam binding for every project in this book, gadget free, then you can adapt as needed.

1. Cut the strips 1½″ wide by length needed.

2. Press both long edges over ¼″, then press the strip in half, resulting in ½″ seam binding.

3. After pressing the seam binding in half, I like to press it again with **Flatter** (page 120), a starch-free smoothing spray. It holds the binding … well … flatter, and makes it so much easier to use!

4. To attach the seam binding, slip the seam binding over the edge to be bound, pin or clip to hold. Stitch in place ⅛″ from the binding edge making sure to catch the bottom layer of binding/tape in the stitches.

Attaching the seam binding / bias binding

Chain Piecing

Chain piecing is an assembly line for your piecing—when you sew your pieces together without snipping the threads before starting the next set of pieces. It is the perfect little time-saver, and saves thread as well!

1. Prepare your pieces, making sure right sides are together, then begin sewing.

2. Once the first set of pieces has passed under the presser foot, take a couple of extra stitches and then feed in the next set. The extra stitches create the chain effect. Easy peasy.

3. You can now either snip all the threads, or use them to keep everything together while you press and then snip!

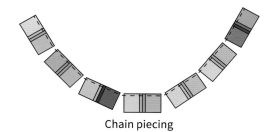
Chain piecing

Chain Piecing Rows

This is the same idea as chain piecing but with a bonus! It makes assembling block-based quilt tops a breeze and is dead handy when you have a block with a lot of pieces that you don't want mixed up!

1. Lay out all the quilt blocks or block pieces in the proper order.

2. Starting on the left side, chain piece all the pieces in the first 2 columns, right sides together. **FIG. A**

3. Flip open. Don't snip the stitches! **FIG. B**

4. Continue sewing the pieces together column-by-column until all the rows are sewn. The rows will be held together by the chain-piecing stitches. No out-of-order blocks! **FIG. C**

5. Press the seams to opposite sides row-by-row, then sew the rows together. You don't need to clip the chain stitches!

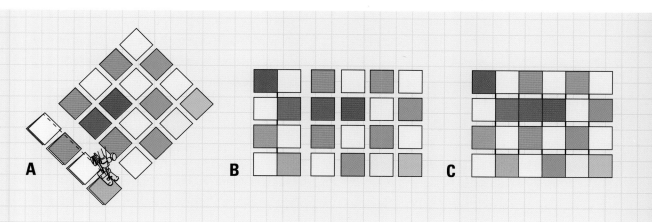

A   B   C

Clipping Corners

Snipping off the little bit of a 90° corner after sewing. This reduces bulk and results in neat corners when you need to turn the corner right side out.

Machine Stitches

Backstitch   Used to secure ends of seams. Sew a couple of stitches forward, press the reverse button on your machine, take a couple stitches back, and then carry on sewing. Repeat when you get to the end.

Bar tack   A very tight zigzag stitch that is used for tacking layers together. Use it in areas that may need extra strength.

Lockstitch   An invisible locking stitch on some sewing machines. Essentially, the machine will drop a couple of stitches on top of each other to lock a seam in place. If your machine doesn't lockstitch, backstitching works just as well!

Overcast stitch   A handy stitch to finish an edge when it doesn't need to be pressed open. If your machine doesn't have an overcast stitch, a zigzag stitch will work just as well. Just make sure to keep it in the seam allowance!

Topstitch   Visible stitching that is used for decorative purposes or to reinforce a seam on the outside of a project. I like to use a stitch length of 3.0 mm, ⅛″ from the edge of a seam. Occasionally I'll stitch 2 rows of topstitching; I like to get crazy sometimes!

Nesting Seams

Nesting seams is a handy little trick that helps your seams to lay flat with the added bonus of working like a locking system to keep your points on point! To nest seams all you need to do is press the seams that will intersect in opposite directions. When it's time to sew them together just place the two seams slightly on top of each other and wiggle the pieces between your fingers until you feel them lock in place. Throw a pin in if you feel so inclined and stitch that seam! Congratulations, you've just nested your seam! I love to use this method when sewing my quilt rows together, with careful sewing I don't need to pin anything and the quilt top comes together in a jiffy!

Piping

Piping is that little bit of fabric covered cording around pillow edges that is just the perfect way to accent your pillow. And when you make the piping yourself, the possibilities are endless for options!

1. To start you need to figure out how wide to cut your fabric strips, which depends on the size of cording. The formula for this is (2 times the cording width) plus (2 times the seam allowance). For example, if your cording is ½″ wide and you're using a ¼″ seam allowance, the formula would be $(2 \times \frac{1}{2}″) + (2 \times \frac{1}{4}″) = 1\frac{1}{2}″$. This means you would cut the strips 1½″ wide.

2. Cut the number of strips required in the instructions and sew them end-to-end with diagonal seams as you would quilt binding. Press the seams open.

3. Fold the strip in half lengthwise, wrong sides together, with the cording sandwiched into fold.

4. Using your zipper foot and with your needle in its regular centered position, baste with the edge of the zipper foot pressed against the cording.

You're now ready to apply your piping!

Making a Template

Depending on the pattern, some templates need to be reused over and over, other times just once. Some templates are used to draw the same shape each time, some are used to cut around. How you are going to use your templates will influence your choice of material to make your template. Paper, card stock, and template plastic are the most common materials. Naturally the template plastic will hold up best under repeated use as a shape to draw around and is also the perfect choice for fabrics that are to be fussy cut! But if straight lines are on the cut list then paper is perfect. Because it's flat you can simply place your ruler over top of the template and cut easily with your rotary cutter. Always make sure to know whether the pattern includes the ¼″ seam allowance or not. This will affect how you cut the fabric, along the edge of the template or ¼″ beyond. Making the template is simple.

1. Gather up your choice of material and have the pattern on hand. In some cases, you may need to tape several sheets of material together.

2. Layer the template material on top of the pattern. Place on a sunny window or use a light box to trace the pattern shape.

3. Cut the shape out on the traced line and now you have a template. Easy peasy, now it's time to cut your fabric!

Quilt Finishing

The magic that happens at the end of the project, where you finally see it all come together. So when you see any version of "layer, quilt, and bind," this is what I mean.

Layer

This refers to layering your quilt top, backing, and batting all together and basting. This is called your quilt sandwich. Yum. This is how I baste my quilts.

1. Spread the batting out on a flat surface. Tape down the corners and sides. Don't stretch the batting out; it just needs to be flat. You don't need to tape the whole perimeter; you just want to be able to move the quilt top around and not have the batting slide all over the place.

2. Lay the quilt top, right side up, on top of the batting. Position it so there's at least 4″ of batting around all 4 sides. Fold back half of the quilt top and, starting in the center, spray baste out toward the edges. Fold the quilt top back down onto the batting and spread it flat. You don't want to stretch the quilt top; it just need to be flat. Keep doing this until you reach the edge of the quilt, then pull back the other side of the quilt top and repeat.

3. I like to trim my batting down to size now. I find it easier to trim once the quilt top is in position than before I start. This way I'm sure that I have enough batting around all 4 sides.

4. Flip it all over so the quilt top is now face down on your hopefully clean floor, and lay the backing down, lining it up with the batting and trimming off any excess. Repeat Step 2 to baste the backing on.

I use 505 Temporary Fabric Adhesive for all my quilt sandwiching. If you are spray basting, open a window or two and maybe stuff some tissue up your nose. That stuff is sticky!

When basting quilts, I generally use a 3″ or 4″ overage of batting on all sides. But for smaller projects like pillows, 2″ is usually more than enough.

Quilt As Desired

I'll be honest and tell you all that the actual quilting part of making a quilt is my least favorite. But I quilt all my own quilts, on my domestic sewing machine, and have since day one. I don't free-motion quilt; I'm a straight-line kinda gal. Well we'll go with "organic straight lines." So for me, my must-have accessory for quilting is my walking foot. It has its own feed dogs, so it pulls the fabrics through evenly for a better finish. I also use my walking foot for topstitching sometimes, and it works great when stitching through thicker fabrics or lots of layers.

For those of you who are new to quilting, there are more online tutorials than you could ever need on all the different ways to quilt your projects! A simple internet search of "free-motion quilting" or "walking-foot quilting" will bring up all kinds of sites from beginner how-tos to advanced techniques! Or maybe you would rather just send your quilt out to be longarm quilted by someone else. There are some truly amazing longarm quilters out there who make serious magic happen with quilting. Or if you're a slow and steady kind of quilter, maybe hand quilting is the way to go. I would hand quilt all my quilts if I could! Try checking out some books too. There are so many amazing quilting books on the market right now, and sometimes isn't it nice to be able to hold an actual book in your hand and learn a new skill? Give one a try, or give them all a try and find out what works best for you!

Bind

We've already discussed types of binding in the binding section, as well as finding out how much you need. So we'll just jump right into how to get your double-fold binding onto your quilt.

1. I like to start about three-quarters of the way down the right-hand side of the quilt. Place the binding strip on the front of the quilt, raw edges aligned with the raw edge of the quilt. Starting down the binding about 6″–8″ (leaving a tail), backstitch then sew forward. Stop ¼″ from the first corner, rotate the quilt a quarter-turn (as if to sew down the next side), and backstitch off the edge of the quilt.

FIG. A

Backstitch off edge.

A

Backstitch off the quilt edge.

2. Remove the quilt from the machine to fold the mitered corner. To do this, fold the binding up at a right angle, keeping the edge of the binding in line with the next edge of the quilt. Now fold the binding back down, again keeping it in line with the quilt edge. Starting from the folded edge begin sewing, backstitching at the start, and continuing on down the side. Repeat the process at every corner, sewing around the perimeter of the quilt and stopping about 15″ from where the binding starts. FIGS. B-C

3. Overlap the binding tails, keeping in line with the quilt edge, and trim the bottom tail so it sits in the middle of the unsewn section. Trim the top tail so the overlap is the same size as the width of the binding strip. FIG. D

4. To join the binding strips, open them both up and place right sides together at a 90° angle. Draw a line from corner to corner, sew on the line, and trim the seam allowance to ¼″. Finger-press the seam allowance open, refold the binding back together, and finish attaching it to the quilt. Backstitch at the start and end. FIG. E

5. Now you just fold over the binding to the back of the quilt and hand stitch down. I like to use a ladder stitch for this.

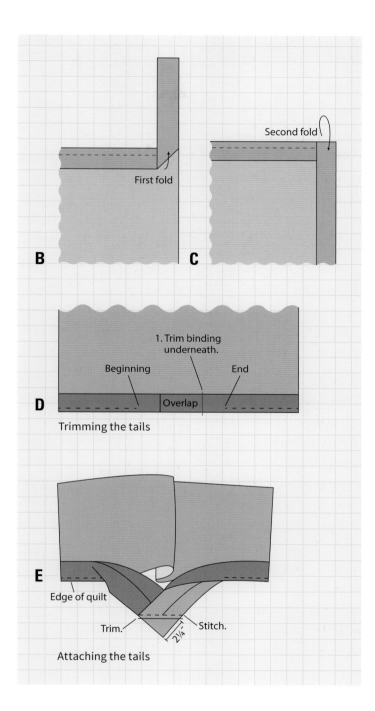

B

First fold

C

Second fold

D   Trimming the tails

Beginning

1. Trim binding underneath.

End

Overlap

E

Edge of quilt

Trim.   2¼″   Stitch.

Attaching the tails

Tools That I Love

Pressing Needs

Pressing is one of my least favorite parts of sewing, but it does need to be done! Here's what I like to use to keep things lying flat.

Flatter (by Soak)   A starch-free smoothing spray made from plant-derived and renewable ingredients, Flatter holds folds like a champ and makes things flatter when pressed. And it's made in Canada—love it!

Seam roller   A tool for rolling seams flat, the seam roller saves on trips to the iron. I roll most of my seams on my blocks as I sew them, only going to the iron when the block is finished. I use Violet Craft's lovely wooden seam roller.

Irons   I'm pretty cheap when it comes to irons. I've never felt the need to spend a few hundred dollars on something that is just going to heat up and flatten things. It could be because I've never used one of the more expensive irons before and maybe I'm missing out. Who knows! So right now I use an old Black+Decker Sure Steam Compact Iron that I "borrowed" from my mom about ten years ago. In my defense, I did leave a brand new iron in its place that I bought and didn't like. I also have a Clover Mini Iron for when I need to get into tight places and to take to classes or retreats.

Keeping It Together

All the tools you need to keep your seams in place and your fabric from shifting!

Wonder Clips (by Clover)   Wonderful little clips that hold everything from zippers, to seams, to superhero capes closed, hair out of your eyes, the gummy bear bag closed, bindings in place … really, there's nothing this little clip can't do. I love the small original size.

Pins   Rarely use them, but when I do, I love Clover's fine patchwork pins. Thin, sharp tips glide easily into fabrics and the heads are made of iron-proof glass.

Fray Check (by Dritz)   That magic little bottle that allows you carry on when you discover that one of your seam allowances somehow slipped to $1/8''$ and the quilt top is already fully assembled. It's a liquid plastic that permanently stops the fabric from fraying. Use it carefully and follow the manufacturer's instructions to the letter.

Fabric glue   I use Roxanne Glue-Baste-It with a needle-nose tip for everything from tricky seams to be matched to holding appliqué in place. It's 100% water soluble, pH neutral and dries clear, and that needle-nose tip is an absolute must have!

MEASURE
ONCE
CUSS
TWICE

Glue sticks   For English paper piecing, I like to use a glue stick. Any kind of washable school glue stick is fine, but I prefer a pen-style glue stick. They're skinnier than a school style glue stick so easier to use without gumming up your project with a lot of extra glue. I'm currently using a Fons & Porter Water-Soluble Fabric Glue Stick Pen and it works wonderfully!

Spray adhesive   I use Odif 505 Temporary Fabric Adhesive for all my quilt basting. It's super-easy to use and for me way quicker than pin basting. It can leave a sticky mess on your floors and it's best to use it in a well-ventilated area, but the drawbacks are few and well worth the time and pain saved from crawling around on my knees pin basting!

Making Your Mark

Marking tools can be extremely handy when you need to mark a point to match something up, or where to start and stop sewing something, or even for quilting lines. Be careful when using any marking tool. Always follow the manufacturer's instructions and whenever possible make your marks in the seam allowance.

Water-soluble pen   This is probably the most common form of temporary marking tool for sewing. Marks are easily removed with water. I don't use water-soluble pens often; I prefer FriXion pens for marking.

FriXion pen (by Pilot)   FriXion pens were not created for use on fabric. Therefore use with caution. I've heard stories of marks coming back with cold temperatures, but thankfully it's never happened to me. FriXion marks are erased with friction, so heat. After you're finished and don't need the mark anymore, you just run your iron over it and magic, it's gone! I do all of my marking that will find its way into the seam allowance with a FriXion pen. I've even mark dots on my quilts for quilting, with a FriXion pen, unless it's on dark fabrics. I have had FriXion pens ghost on dark prints before. Meaning that after I ran my iron over the ink to make it disappear, there was a whitish mark where the line was. Yikes! So for dark fabrics I like to use a fabric chalk pencil.

Chalk pencil   Essentially chalk, in pencil form. Can sometimes be messy and some types contain wax, so make sure you check before you use it.

Hera Marker (by Clover)   This marker has a sharp edge that leaves a temporary crease after dragging it across the fabric. After my FriXion pen, a Hera Marker is my favorite marking tool. This is the one I use for any quilt lines that I make, especially when hand quilting.

Masking tape   Yep, good old masking tape, perfect for laying down lines to use as guide for quilting. Peel it up and stick it down again. Just be careful the tape doesn't leave a sticky residue after peeling it off. Painters tape is a low-tack masking tape that is perfect for this!

Measure Once, Cuss Twice

For all my fabric cutting needs, these are my go-to tools!

Cutting mat   I have been cutting on the same 24″ × 36″ OLFA cutting mat my parents bought me more than 20 years ago. And it's still in great shape! I also love my 12″ OLFA rotating cutting mat, super-handy that one!

Rotary cutter   My parents also bought me OLFA's 45 mm deluxe handle rotary cutter to go with that mat and it's still the only rotary cutter

I use! (Occasionally I will use a 28 mm rotary cutter when working with curves.) Obviously not the same blade, but the rotary cutter itself has definitely withstood the test of time. For blades I swear by OLFA's Endurance blades. They cost a little more than their regular blades, but it is surprising how much longer they last!

Scissors   I have been using an inexpensive pair of Havel scissors that I won in a contest years ago and they still cut like a hot knife through butter! The trick with scissors is to use them only for fabric. Nothing else. Even when the paper scissors have been stolen by little hands and are in another room and your fabric scissors are just hanging there, doing nothing. Don't use them! They are for fabric only!

Pinking shears   The funny scissors that cut little notches out of your fabric. These are super-handy to have on hand as an alternative to clipping notches around curves (the notches help ease the fabric so it lies flat). Or when you don't want to overcast an edge to finish it. The notches cut will keep the fabric from fraying. This can also be useful if you prewash your fabrics. Just trim all unfinished sides with the pinking shears and when the fabric comes out of the wash you won't have that monster ball of thread that tangles everything together!

Acrylic rulers   I'm not loyal to one brand of rulers. I have rulers made by Omnigrid, Creative Grids, and Quilter's Select, plus some specialty rulers. There are three sizes that get the most use above all. My 6″ × 24″ is my go-to when I need to cut yardage. Next would be my 6″ × 12″, because as handy as the 24″-long ruler is, it can be troublesome when you need small pieces.

And, I think my most used ruler is my 6½″ square ruler. That thing has squared up more half-square triangles than stars in the sky! Okay, okay, maybe not that many, though it sure feels like it in the moment!

Threading the Needle

I'm pretty particular when it comes to my thread, but more laid back with my needles. It's all about balance, right?!

Bobbin thread for piecing   I use DecoBob (by Wonderfil Specialty Threads) in my bobbin. I use the white or the dove gray for everything. This is an 80-weight polyester thread, so for all the cotton thread purists out there, this isn't the one for you. But you may want to try it—it's such a fine thread that it doesn't eat up your seam allowance, which you wouldn't think would make too much of a difference. But when micro-piecing a 5″ block with 81 pieces, you'd be surprised what you lose in the seam allowances! The only time I take the DecoBob out is when I'm quilting and I need a different color. But I have quilted with them in my bobbin and as a top thread and the results are fantastic. They just disappear and let the piecework of the quilt shine.

Top thread for piecing   Most of my piecing is done with Aurifil 50-weight 2600 Dove (gray). I've never once had a problem with Aurifil's threads and recommend them to anyone. I do switch out the Aurifil with InvisaFil (by Wonderfil Specialty Threads) when foundation paper piecing or micro piecing, though. I find that the finer thread leads to less bulk in the seams, which can make a huge difference when using pieces that are extremely tiny or when foundation piecing. Less bulk in your seams equals more accurate finished blocks!

Thread for machine quilting   I like to mix it up. Aurifil is always going to be tops for me, but I have been using Cotton + Steel thread (by Sulky) with some wonderful results and also playing with a bit with Hemingworth embroidery thread to see how it quilts up. It is a polyester thread so there's that, but I've had some beautiful results with it. Be sure to test your thread out in your machine first though; some machines just don't like certain types of thread.

Thread for hand quilting   I use Aurifil 12-weight almost exclusively for hand quilting. It is the perfect weight for hand quilting and the range of colors is staggering.

Thread wax   A necessity in my sewing arsenal, it conditions the thread and helps prevent tangles and knots. I use it when hand quilting as well as when I English paper piece. I'm currently working through a stash of Thread Heaven that I grabbed when I found they were stopping production of it, but I also have a tin of Sew Fine Thread Gloss that I will be permanently switching to when my Thread Heaven is all gone, or maybe sooner … there are so many different scents of Sew Fine and they are all soooo good!

Machine needles   I use the same needle for everything. I keep a Schmetz quilting 75/11 needle (it has a smaller blade and is designed for piecing) in my machine almost permanently. I will sometimes switch it out to a quilting 90/14 needle, which is designed to be used with a slightly thicker thread for quilting. But I do this only if I decide to move from a 50-weight piecing thread to a 40-weight or 28-weight for quilting.

I always use a new needle for a new quilt, sometimes more than one. Did you know the average lifespan of a needle is only about 6 to 8 hours? But otherwise the

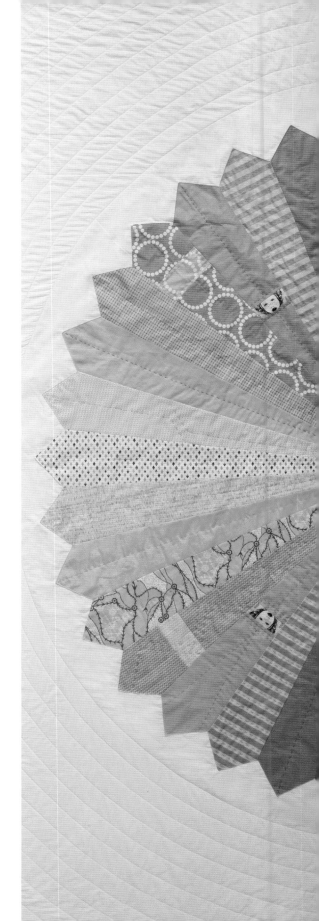

only time I switch my needle is if I'm going to be sewing through something heavy-duty and need a denim needle. Or on the odd occasion when I topstitch with a heavier thread (12-weight), in which case I will use a topstitch needle. I don't work with a lot of different types of fabrics, so I don't really have a need for all the different types of needles. But if you are going to be sewing with a specific type of fabric or nonstandard type of thread (think metallic!) a quick internet search will give you all the information you need on the best needle for your project!

Hand-sewing needles   For English paper piecing, I like to use a milliners #10 needle, usually John James. I use Black Gold Needles Quilting Between #10 (by Clover) for hand quilting. I also keep a mixed pack size 3/9 of quilting needles from John James for big-stitch hand quilting. The eye is larger in these, which allows the thicker thread to pass through more easily. I like a thin needle for hand stitching my bindings down, and usually use the same milliners needle that I use for English paper piecing. But there are so many more types of needles out there that I still need to try! It's another one of those tools that you need to just keep trying until you find the ones you like.

Thread snips   I have two pairs of thread snips that I absolutely love. I use Tula Pink's EZ Snip for when I'm at my machine. I love everything about these little snips, from the serrated blades for precise cutting to the curved handle that allows the snips to work like they were spring loaded. And they look pretty awesome too! When I'm hand sewing, I keep a pair of Gingher 4″ embroidery scissors handy in my sewing kit. They're super-sharp and the perfect size for snipping threads. And the little leather protective case they come with keeps them from accidently poking through your sewing kit, or heaven forbid into your couch (*ahem!*).

Tools Not Easily Categorized but Equally Important

Seam gauge   A short ruler (usually about 6″ long) that has a sliding marker on it that works wonders when you need to measure the same distance repeatedly. I use mine most often when folding hems for seam bindings and such.

Seam ripper   The tool in your arsenal that will undoubtedly see the most use. I use a simple Clover seam ripper with a plastic handle and replace it fairly often. They do eventually get dull. Use carefully and go slowly, there's nothing worse than ripping a seam out and accidentally ripping into your fabric!

Hermione's wand   You know, for summoning snacks, *accio* snacks! Freezing the kids when they fight … *Petrificus totalus!* Floating quilt blocks up onto the design wall … *Wingardium leviosa!* Okay, in all seriousness, this isn't a proper tool, it's a toy, but I actually do use Hermione's wand in my sewing room for pushing blocks flat on my design wall in the upper corner that I can't reach. Sadly, no magic.

Pointy tweezers   I like to keep a pair of needle-nose tweezers in my sewing room. They're helpful when you need to gently coerce fabric from under the presser foot of your machine, or for holding tricky bits when feeding fabric into your machine. Or sometimes just for helping to get the jackrabbit-size dust bunnies from your bobbin casing and surrounding area.

Chopstick   I like to use a chopstick for gently pushing out corners when turning things right side out. I've used a pencil in a pinch, but you run the risk of getting lead on your fabric or, even worse, pushing the tip of the pencil right through. A chopstick has a nice blunt tip that is just perfect.

Quilting gloves   A must-have for helping move the fabric while quilting. I use a really basic pair that is essentially a pair of stretchy gloves with little rubber nubs for grip. But they do make all kinds of fancy gloves with special features that help reduce wrist strain and vibrations. If you're a nonglove quilter, give a pair a try. You may be pleasantly surprised at how much easier it is quilt with them!

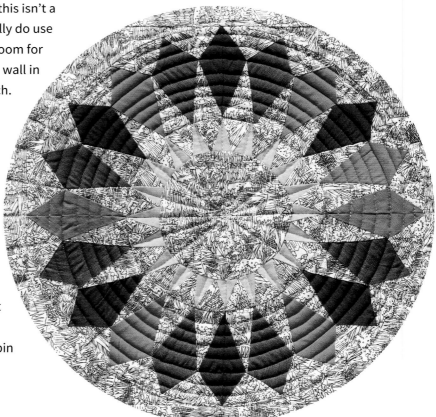

ABOUT THE AUTHOR

Nicole Calver is a self-taught quilter who never in her life would have guessed she'd be quilting full-time for a living! With a background in street art and graffiti-style painting, Nicole came to quilting after the birth of her first son in 2010. Two boys (and a few years) later, and she's developed a signature style that combines her love of color (all the colors!) and print with a cutting-edge design sensibility.

Nicole lives just outside Toronto, Ontario, with her husband, two little guys, and Dottie, the dog.

Visit Nicole online and follow on social media!

Blog: snipssnippets.ca

Instagram: @snipssnippets

Photo by Nicole Calver

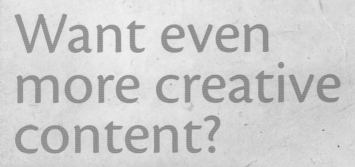

Want even more creative content?

Go to ctpub.com/offer

& sign up to receive our gift to you!

Make it,
snap it,
share it
using
#ctpublishing

By Day and By Night Quilt

Mega Dresden Plate

Two-Face Pill

Medium Dres